The Master Musicians Series

BRUCKNER

Series edited by
Sir Jack Westrup, MA, HonDMus(Oxon), FRCO
Professor Emeritus of Music, Oxford University

VOLUMES IN THE MASTER MUSICIANS SERIES

Bach *Eva Mary and Sydney Grew*
Bartók *Lajos Lesznai*
Beethoven *Marion M. Scott*
Bellini *Leslie Orrey*
Berlioz *J. H. Elliot*
Brahms *Peter Latham*
Bruckner *Derek Watson*
Chopin *Arthur Hedley*
Debussy *Edward Lockspeiser*
Delius *Alan Jefferson*
Dvořák *Alec Robertson*
Elgar *Ian Parrott*
Franck *Laurence Davies*
Grieg *John Horton*
Handel *Percy M. Young*
Haydn *Rosemary Hughes*
Liszt *Walter Beckett*
Mahler *Michael Kennedy*
Mendelssohn *Philip Radcliffe*
Monteverdi *Denis Arnold*
Mozart *Eric Blom*
Mussorgsky *M. D. Calvocoressi*
Purcell *Sir Jack Westrup*
Schubert *Arthur Hutchings*
Schumann *Joan Chissell*
Sibelius *Robert Layton*
Smetana *John Clapham*
Tchaikovsky *Edward Garden*
Vaughan Williams *James Day*
Verdi *Dyneley Hussey*
Wagner *Robert L. Jacobs*

IN PREPARATION

Berg *Nicholas Chadwick*
Prokofiev *Rita McAllister*
Ravel *Roger Nichols*
Rakhmaninov *Geoffrey Norris*
Schoenberg *Malcolm MacDonald*
Richard Strauss *Michael Kennedy*
Stravinsky *Francis Routh*
Tallis and Byrd *Michael Howard*

THE MASTER MUSICIANS SERIES

BRUCKNER

by Derek Watson

With eight pages of plates and music examples in the text

J. M. DENT & SONS LTD
LONDON

First published 1975

Made in Great Britain
at the
Aldine Press · Letchworth · Herts
for
J. M. DENT & SONS LTD
Aldine House · Albemarle Street · London

This book is set in 11 on 12 pt Fournier 185

Hardback ISBN 0 460 03144 9
Paperback ISBN 0 460 02171 0

Preface

There is no parallel to Bruckner among creative artists. Perhaps a fellow symphonist, Shostakovich, has an affinity in so far as he is also an outwardly shy and unheroic personality who none the less speaks heroically in his scores. Bruckner's contemporaries failed miserably in their attempt to comprehend him—neither their erroneous conception of his music as symphonic Wagnerianism nor their pitting of his talents against those of the symphonist Brahms helps us even slightly towards an understanding of his genius. The enigma of Bruckner's personality, coupled with the 'difficulty' of his idiom, long beclouded attempts at serious interest in him outside Austria and Germany. In 1938 Sir Henry J. Wood wrote: 'On October 15 [1903] I produced Bruckner's seventh symphony. This was its first and last performance at the Promenades. The public would not have it then; neither will they now.' Two decades later this situation was quite reversed, and my distinguished predecessor in this series, Hans F. Redlich, wrote in the preface to the 1963 edition of *Bruckner and Mahler* of the marked increase of interest in both composers throughout the Western Hemisphere.

As I write a decade later still, and on the eve of the 150th anniversary of Bruckner's birth, it is gratifying to find almost every significant work of his available on disc, including a number of his early works and his smallest motets, many of them appearing on several labels. And, *pace* Sir Henry, that most enterprising and innovatory of English conductors, I have heard the very symphony that was disdained by the public of his day receive more than one ovation at the Promenades. 'Patience et longueur de temps/Font plus que force ni que rage', says La Fontaine's couplet. Patience was Bruckner's greatest virtue in his slow, monumental unfolding. Passage of time has justified his patience. Like every other artist, Bruckner will no doubt continue to have his detractors. To those who are on the threshold of his music for the first time there is one word of encouragement and advice—patience.

Every biographer of Bruckner is indebted to the diligent researches of August Göllerich and Max Auer, to whom I add my own tribute and acknowledgment. I should like to express my thanks to all those who have lent encouragement, helpful advice and practical assistance to the preparation of this book, especially Mr Deryck Cooke, Dr Robert Simpson, Miss Eileen Skinner and Mr Ronald Stevenson.

My gratitude also to Mrs Joan James who typed my manuscript; to my parents who helped me see it through the press; and to Argo Records, C.B.S. Records, Music for Pleasure Ltd and Oryx Recordings Ltd for their assistance. Music examples appear by kind permission of Boosey and Hawkes, London, on behalf of the copyright owners.

Edinburgh, 1974. D. W.

Contents

Illustrations

TO EILEEN

1 Childhood in Upper Austria

Austria in the decades leading up to the revolution of 1848, that is during the period known as the *Vormärz*, was a living example of feudalism. The various arms of the state wielded complete control and the official language with its stiff, formal, stereotyped phrases was characteristic of a period of deepest reaction and intolerance. Metternich's reactionary empire contained groups of the most primitive people in European society, and the Catholic peasantry were quite unaffected by the growing liberalism and sophistication of life that was occurring elsewhere in Europe. The iron grip of the State was reinforced by the authority of the Roman Catholic Church, which held the unswerving devotion of the peasantry.

Born during the reign of the Emperor Francis I (1768–1835) Joseph Anton Bruckner was a child of the *Vormärz*, and the environment and educational system of those years stamped his character for life. His birthplace, Ansfelden, is near Linz in the Traun district of Upper Austria. The river Danube flows through Upper Austria from the Bavarian city of Passau in the west and passes by Linz, the capital of the region, which was over two hours' journey from Ansfelden. The countryside around Ansfelden, bordered by the rivers Traun and Enns, presents a rich landscape of streams, valleys, meadows and woods and contains two medieval cathedral towns, Enns and Steyr, and shelters resplendent monasteries. Within view of the Salzburg Alps in the west, this fertile area was exclusively peasant farming land.

The innumerable amusing anecdotes about the oddities of

Bruckner's character can be explained if not disposed of by a few moments' reflection on these social and geographical factors of which he was a product. In an era when agnosticism gripped the thoughts of intellectuals and artists throughout Europe, he remained an unquestioning believer. Towards the end of a century that had begun with Beethoven scorning his patrons, Bruckner always remained humble in attitude to his superiors. In fashionable Vienna, where he spent almost the last thirty years of his life, he raised eyebrows and added spice to the pages of generations of biographers by retaining his Upper Austrian habits of dress, speech and cautious manner. Countless quaint characteristics persisted that had their origins in his formative years prior to 1848, and the most important result of them was that as an artist he also stood outside the accepted boundaries of nineteenth-century Romanticism. These characteristics have been so often repeated and so much exaggerated that there has arisen the case for Anton Bruckner, the country bumpkin. The rest of this book proposes to demolish that case.

Research has shown that the Bruckner family had lived in the vicinity of Linz for over four centuries before Anton's birth. Jörg Pruckner, a feudal peasant born around 1400, had a holding near Oed (twenty-five miles east of Linz) called the *Pruckhof*, and the family name derives from their living near a bridge—*Brücke*, or, in old Austrian, *Pruck*. Josef Bruckner, born in Pyhra near Oed in 1715, acquired some wealth by marriage and in leaving the family home turned from a long line of peasants and farmers who had prospered for a time, had owned quarries, had even in a few cases become aldermen and acquired nobility, and established himself in Oed as a house-owner, innkeeper and broom-maker. One of his sons, another Joseph (1749–1831), followed in the trade of broom-making but married a schoolmaster's daughter, Franziska Kletzer, and finally took up teaching and was posted to Ansfelden in 1776. The tenth of his twelve children, Anton, born in 1791, became his father's assistant and, in 1823, his successor. In the same year he married Therese Helm (born 1801), the daughter of Ferdinand Helm, a civil servant and innkeeper from Neuzeug near Steyr. Of their eleven children, five survived infancy.

Thus their eldest son Tonerl (the diminutive form of Anton in Upper Austrian dialect), born on 4th September 1824, was, like Schubert, a schoolmaster's son. The position of schoolmaster was the most respected one in the village next to that of priest, but in reality it meant a hard life with many extra duties and a miserable salary. One of the extra duties was to act as church organist and, so it seems, Tonerl's favourite place in church was next to his father on the organ bench. His mother, who had a fine singing voice and sang in the church choir, took the boy with her to High Mass from earliest childhood. At the church was an 'orchestra' of two violins, one double bass, clarinet and horn, except on special occasions when two trumpeters and a timpanist were brought from Linz. The music of the day stemmed from the graduals and offertories for the liturgical year written by Michael Haydn for the Archbishop Hieronymus of Salzburg, which were taken by other composers as models to be followed. By the age of four Tonerl was playing a few hymns on the violin and not long after trying his father's spinet. The elder Bruckner was an enthusiastic musician and did everything to stimulate the talent that began to appear in his son—the only one of his first four children to survive.

At ten the boy was able to deputize for his father at the organ, and by that time he had come to know what was to remain his lifelong spiritual home, the Augustinian monastery of St Florian. The journey to Linz being too long, visits to St Florian with its magnificent organ and opulent baroque architecture were frequent for the family.

By the spring of 1835 Tonerl had three younger sisters, Rosalie, Josefa and Maria Anna ('Nani'), and a young brother, Ignaz. The eldest son was therefore sent from the crowded house to live with his godfather and cousin Johann Baptist Weiss, schoolteacher and organist at Hörsching. Weiss was a genuine artistic personality and the composer of a number of sacred works, including a Requiem in E♭ major [1] which shows an individual and strongly devotional spirit. In his later years Bruckner expressed his lasting spiritual indebtedness to this man who gave him his first serious tuition in harmony, figured bass and organ playing. This beneficial period which lasted until December 1836 also introduced him to a wider repertory of church music, including Mozart's Masses and Haydn's *Creation* and *The Seasons*, improved his general education and saw his first attempts at composition: a short, neatly shaped, homophonic 'Pange lingua' in C major, which probably dates from this time; a work for chorus and instruments referred to by Bruckner on 14th July 1835 but now lost; and four organ preludes which display daring if not academically sound harmonic imagination. The 'Pange lingua', where classical models are strongly evident, spans Bruckner's entire creative career, as he revised it as late as 1891.

The close of 1836 saw Tonerl's father seriously ill and brought the twelve-year-old boy back to Ansfelden, where he took over some of his father's duties. These had proved a great strain for the older man's health—which is not surprising as his duties as sexton involved ringing church bells at four or five in the morning, and he often worked well into the night playing the fiddle at village dances to augment his meagre income. Tonerl saw his father die of consumption on 7th June 1837, and that very day his mother took him to St Florian to ask the prior, Michael Arneth, to accept him as a chorister. Arneth, who was interested in music and who often entertained the brothers Anton and Franz von Spaun, intimate friends of Schubert, admitted the boy and from that time on was his staunch supporter and friend. Bruckner's mother moved to Ebelsberg with her four children.

[1] Published by Ernst Lanninger, 1892.

St Florian, ten miles from Linz, is an ancient monastery which dates in its present form from 1686 to 1751. The architect was Carlo Carlone and the building was completed under the supervision of Jacob Prandtauer and Jacob Steinhuber. Nestling in the terraces of the Upper Austrian hills, it is one of Austria's finest examples of Baroque architecture, and not only was it to shelter Bruckner in his days as a scholar but also throughout his career remained his retreat from the world, and represents much of what characterizes Bruckner the man and artist. Baroque splendour, the high towers, the hundreds of windows, the elegant marble, the paintings, the treasures of the library and, above all, the *Stiftkirche* itself with its three organs made a profound impression on the boy which should not be underrated. The great organ (now known as the 'Bruckner Organ') was built by Krismann in 1771 and had about seventy stops. Tonerl's education continued with lessons in reading, writing and arithmetic and included organ and piano lessons from the noted organist Anton Kattinger, violin lessons from Gruber (a pupil of Beethoven's friend Schuppanzigh) and studies in musical theory. Figured-bass lessons were given by the headmaster, Bogner, in whose home Tonerl lodged with two other choirboys. When he was fourteen official schooling ended and more time was spent at the organ, particularly at the practice of improvisation. A year later Tonerl's voice broke and although replaced in the choir he continued to take an active part for a while in music-making at St Florian, both as violinist and as deputy organist for certain minor services.

The time came for deciding on a career. Bruckner seems to have been guided by the axiom 'like father, like son' and accordingly he was prepared for the *Präparandie* (teacher-training school) in Linz, and passed the entrance examination on 1st October 1840. Already he seems to have considered financial prospects and the welfare of his mother and family carefully and conscientiously, and this may have had some bearing on his choice of profession. The ten-month course in Linz included plenty of musical studies as the custom in villages ordained that schoolmasters were responsible for music in the church. His teacher was J. N. August Dürrnberger, author of a book on musical theory to which Bruckner later said he owed all, and which he used as the basis of his own teaching in his Vienna years. The activity of the provincial capital must have been a sharp contrast to the quietness of his boyhood villages and the seclusion of St Florian. Musical horizons too were widened. Dürrnberger introduced him to Bach's *Die Kunst der Fuge* and the fugues of Albrechtsberger. While the worldly pleasures of the theatre were denied to students of the *Präparandie* Bruckner absorbed more and more Viennese classical church music, especially the works of Joseph and Michael Haydn and those of minor figures such as Zenetti, Keinsdorfer and Schiedermayer. The repertory at St Florian included Albrechtsberger, Aumann, Eybler, Aiblinger, Zaininger, Bühler, Caldara and of course Gregorian chant. But secular music found its place too, and the secular concerts at St Florian together with the meetings of the Linz Music Association had already brought to his attention overtures and small works by Rossini, Beethoven, Weber and Mendelssohn, together with a few symphonies by Mozart and Beethoven.

Bruckner was a model student, doing well in his final examination in Linz which qualified him as 'assistant teacher for elementary schools'—a fine achievement, as most students took two attempts at the course before gaining a certificate. He then spent a few weeks at St Florian, possibly also visiting his family at Ebelsberg, and his official student days were over.

2 Years of apprenticeship

In October 1841 Bruckner was appointed assistant teacher in Windhaag, a small village of about thirty-five houses by the Bohemian border and near Freystadt. On the whole this was a time of servile drudgery for the young assistant, who found himself bound to a hard master, the teacher Fuchs, overloaded with menial tasks and subject to many humiliations. He consequently regarded Windhaag with much the same feelings that Mozart had held for Salzburg. Life followed the pattern of his father's, beginning each day by tolling the morning bell at 4 a.m., and frequently playing the violin at village dances to augment his wage of twelve florins per annum. Out of this paltry sum the seventeen-year-old boy, already remarkably cautious, paid his first contribution to an insurance policy for his old age. He turned for consolation to the things that he was always to revere—his religion, the church organ and his composition, completing a short Mass in C major for solo contralto, accompanied by the poor forces he had available: organ and two horns. He continued his studies of *Die Kunst der Fuge* and the fugues of Albrechtsberger and found a friendly, musical family, that of the weaver Sücka, with whom he formed a band, in which he played second fiddle at country inns for wedding entertainments and other celebrations.

When Arneth came to Windhaag on a tour of inspection, Fuchs took the opportunity to express his extreme dissatisfaction with Bruckner, who had particularly irked him by failing to do manual duties in the fields such as shifting manure, and who had further upset him by showing such keen musical ambitions. Arneth reacted in effect with a kind of promotion rather than a punishment and Bruckner found himself transferred to Kronstorf on 23rd January 1843. A much happier time ensued in the houes of his superior, Franz S. Lehofer, and his wife, and Bruckner always remembered them with affection. The village, situated between Enns and Steyr, was half the size of Windhaag and just within walking distance of St Florian, to which Bruckner was a frequent visitor. Soon his salary was raised to twenty florins. His Kronstorf days involved much music-making with new friends and he sang in a male-voice choir. Through the kindness of a farmer, Josef Födermayer, he had placed in his classroom an old spinet on which he practised Bach.

In Enns Bruckner renewed his acquaintance with the fine organist and choirmaster Leopold Edler von Zenetti, whom he had known at St Florian, and took lessons from him three times a week in musical theory. Zenetti's teaching was based on the textbook of D. G. Türk and the chorales and 'Well-tempered Clavier' of Bach. Bruckner also made good friends with the priest in Steyr and this gave him the opportunity of practising on the fine Krismann organ there. Steyr was to be another spiritual retreat for him in his later years, and so to the influence of Baroque architecture was added that of the Renaissance and Gothic ages for which Steyr is noted, in particular the great German Gothic *Stadtpfarrkirche*. Also in Steyr he met Karoline Eberstaller, the daughter of a French general. She had played duets with Schubert whenever he stayed in Steyr in the last years of his life, and now she introduced Bruckner to his piano duets which they played together.

Composition developed during the Kronstorf years. Two secular works, *Vergissmeinnicht* (1845) and *An dem Feste* (1843), were later revised by Bruckner, the latter as late as 1893 when it was renamed *Tafellied*. The sacred choral works of this period are much influenced by classical models and show that he had securely grasped the principles of composition, but so far without any clear individuality. Apart from additional musical studies, organ practice, music-making, composition, and his heavy rota of official duties, he was occupied in preparing for an examination (the *Konkursprüfung*) which every assistant teacher had to pass four years after his initial qualification. Again he achieved this with marked success on 29th May 1845 and even surprised his old teacher Dürrnberger by the quality of his contrapuntal improvisation at the organ. He was now a fully equipped school-teacher.

St Florian had a vacancy for an assistant teacher and Bruckner found himself back there in that capacity on 25th September with a salary of thirty-six florins per annum and filling the role of deputy organist to his former teacher Kattinger. For a decade he taught the lowest two classes in the school and music was of necessity a leisure-time activity throughout this period. Nevertheless he maintained his organ practice for two hours each day under Kattinger's supervision, concentrating on improvisation and the works of Bach, and frequently travelled to hear recitals in Linz. He now worked through Marpurg's *Treatise on the Fugue* in a new edition by Simon Sechter. Compositions of this time were largely for chorus and included a Requiem of 1845 (now lost) for his friend Deschl, schoolmaster at Kirchberg. The organ music which has survived is unimportant, and probably none of his works at this time reflect his growing skill at improvisation. The male-voice choruses he wrote were the result of his singing first bass in a newly formed male quartet. The second bass was the gardener at St Florian, Johann Nepomuk Huebler, who was to marry Bruckner's sister Rosalie and later settle with her in Vöcklabruck. In 1847 Bruckner was deeply impressed on hearing Mendelssohn's *St Paul* in Linz, and the influence of Mendelssohn on his work became marked.

Throughout his teaching days at St Florian he stayed again in the house of the headmaster Bogner, and was much attracted to the daughter of the house, Louise; but the romance came to nothing, leaving its mark only in the songs and piano pieces of these years. The godfather of Bruckner's brother Ignaz, Franz Sailer, a judicial actuary, bought a Bösendorfer grand piano and Bruckner had access to this fine instrument. In 1848 Sailer had a sudden heart attack and died, and this had two important results. The first was that Bruckner inherited the Bösendorfer piano, which he used throughout his life, and the second was the beginning of a work in grateful memory of his benefactor, the Requiem in D minor, completed in 1849 and first performed at St Florian on 13th March of that year—a landmark in his creative career and his first truly notable large work.

The year of revolutions, 1848, affected Bruckner and St Florian mildly. Bruckner enrolled in the National Guard and took part in some military exercises. More important, Kattinger was transferred to Kremsmünster and Bruckner became provisional organist—his first step towards a professional musical career. It seems to have disquieted him and awakened indecisiveness: dissatisfaction with his teaching life and a growing longing for a musical profession conflicting with his dependence on a financially secure position. It was the beginning of a spell of unhappiness and fretfulness that overshadowed his remaining years at St Florian. He even applied for the position of a clerk in the civil service for which he claimed to feel a vocation, pointing out that he had been studying Latin and physics; but to the great benefit of musical history this particular application was unsuccessful, although he did work as a voluntary clerk at the local Court and acquired some legal knowledge. He also added a testimonial for Latin studies to his growing collection of certificates.

In 1850 Bruckner was saddened and shocked to learn of the fate of his godfather and former teacher Weiss. Innocently Weiss had accepted the responsibility for a church fund from which, unknown to him, a large sum had been embezzled. On the morning of 10th July a police officer approached his cottage and the poor, terrified man fled to the graveyard and killed himself. Bruckner tried several times in vain to persuade the church authorities to entrust to him the skull of his revered relative, and it is a sign of the affection he felt for him that as late as 1895 the ailing composer wrote the last of many requests to the church authorities at Hörsching for a Mass to be said for the repose of Weiss's soul.

Bruckner embarked upon a two-year course at this time to improve his general eduction, at the *Unter-Realschule* of Linz, preparatory to becoming a high-school teacher. While his salary rose as provincial organist and he became entitled to free board and lodging, his unhappiness continued—an unsuccessful love-affair with a sixteen-year-old girl, Antonie Werner, and about the same time a criticism from his colleagues for devoting too little energy to teaching and too much to music. This censure hurt the conscientious Bruckner and he was not placated until he had obtained a written testimonial from his superiors confirming his good conduct and reliable character, and a written guarantee from Arneth assuring his salary. He wrote at this time to his successor-to-be as organist at St Florian, Josef Seiber: 'You see how everything has altered. I sit in my small room, all alone and in the deepest melancholy.'

In 1851 Bruckner paid a visit to Vienna to see Ignaz Assmayer, court conductor, notable composer of sacred music, pupil of Michael Haydn and friend of Schubert. To him he wrote in the following year, complaining bitterly of his life at St Florian and of the lack of interest in music there. In 1852 he completed settings of Psalm 114 (dedicated to Assmayer) and Psalm 22, and of an impressive Magnificat in B flat major. Mendelssohn and the Viennese classics were still his principal models, and in an interesting letter of July 1853 his friend Schaarschmidt advised him to give up the idea of becoming a civil servant or of changing his job and continued: 'You are making a mistake if you look exclusively to Mendelssohn for your instruction. In any case you should take from the sources he did, that is Sebastian Bach, whom you should study thoroughly.'

On 24th March Bruckner's friend Michael Arneth died. After the Requiem Mass two works were sung that were specially written by the thirty-year-old composer, whose career he had aided so much: *By Arneth's Grave* and a 'Libera' in F minor. In August his Magnificat was first heard at St Florian and a week later the Missa Solennis in B flat minor was completed. This Mass, which is the most important milestone between the Requiem of 1849 and the great choral works of the 1860s, was first performed at the enthroning of Arneth's successor, Friedrich Mayer, on 14th September and aroused much enthusiasm. Bruckner was slighted by the fact that no one asked him to the banquet which followed the ceremony. The tale is told that he took himself off to a nearby inn, ordered a lonely but ample meal of five courses with three different wines, and began his private celebration with the words, '*That* Mass deserves it!' More achievements followed in the form of further certificates—one for passing an organ examination in Vienna on 9th October at which he improvised a double fugue before Assmayer, Sechter and Preyer, and the other of January 1855 for passing his examination for the qualification of high-school teacher at Linz, with 'very good' in all subjects.

Robert Führer, an organist from Prague, arrived in St Florian in 1855 and Bruckner showed him his Missa Solennis and improvised on the organ. Führer gave him an excellent testimonial and advised him to take lessons in strict harmony and counterpoint with the Viennese teacher Simon Sechter. As Mayer had given similar advice to him after hearing the Mass, Bruckner set off in July with the work and Führer's reference. Sechter immediately accepted the applicant as a pupil but advised him to leave St Florian—advice that made him more agitated than ever about his future. He began to look around for a post as musician and secretly and unsuccessfully applied for the post of organist at Olmütz (Olomouc) Cathedral; but this action brought him a sharp censure from the prior at St Florian.

Simon Sechter was born in 1788 in Friedberg, Bohemia, and lived in Vienna from 1804. In 1824 he became Voříšek's successor as court organist. In 1828 Schubert, within weeks of his death, approached him for counterpoint lessons and in 1850 he was appointed a professor of composition at the Vienna Conservatorium. His pupils included Thalberg and Vieuxtemps and he was the composer of oratorios, Masses, operas (including a burlesque opera *Ali hitsch-hatsch*), organ music and over 5,000 fugues. Sechter was a profound thinker and an energetic, diligent craftsman who wrote at least one fugue a day. His interests included numerology, as seen in his '104 Variations on a theme of 104 bars' (which is a tantalizingly curious pointer to Bruckner's later numeromania and might well indicate an affinity between the two men). Sechter was a naturally generous man and through his own kindness reduced himself to poverty in his last years. As a teacher he was the author of a three-volume treatise, *The Principles of Musical Composition* (1853–5), based on a Rameau-inspired theory of 'inter-dominants'.[1] Bruckner thoroughly mastered Sechter's rigorous system, which was exclusively a study of the music of the past (figures such as Marpurg, Türk, Kirnberger and of course Rameau), and it is possible that this found a practical outlet in the harmonic clarity, advanced modulations and striking tonal contrasts of his mature works.

But the strict discipline of the years with Sechter may have had a more significant result. All Bruckner's works prior to this time are competent, orthodox and in some cases highly effective,

[1] Rameau first set down the theory of the fundamental bass, the basic root of each chord and its inversions. A systematic progression by intervals of 4ths or 5ths of these roots, which need not be audible or sounded, governs the rules of modulation.

but they give little or no hint of the outburst of originality that shortly followed. Perhaps Bruckner laboured so hard at orthodox procedures while studying with Sechter (a period almost totally devoid of original compositions) that he worked them out of his system and cleared the way for new thoughts. Robert Simpson has written:[1] 'It is possible that Sechter unknowingly brought about Bruckner's originality by insisting that it be suppressed until it could no longer be contained.' In any sphere it is not uncommon for something to work itself to an extreme pitch, fall away exhausted and give way to something new and fresh. It is the pattern of many steps in musical history and it suggests that Bruckner's years with Simon Sechter formed an important bridge to the awakening of his art—a bridge that no other composer had crossed in quite the same way.

[1] *The Essence of Bruckner* (Gollancz, 1967).

3 Linz

In November 1855 the post of cathedral organist in Linz became vacant and on the 13th of the month a preliminary examination of candidates took place. On that morning the organ-tuner arrived at St Florian and expressed surprise that Bruckner was not in Linz to apply for the position. He was reluctantly cajoled into going to Linz, where he called upon Dürrnberger. He was hesitant about taking the examination, fearing both the future and the opinion of his superiors at St Florian, but accompanied Dürrnberger to listen to the other applicants, both of whom, it transpired, failed to satisfy the examiners in providing a fugal improvisation on a set theme. Dürrnberger approached Bruckner, who was praying, and insisted: 'Tonerl, you *must* play!' Bruckner then sat at the organ and improvised with such skill and contrapuntal mastery that the result of the competition was obvious. On hearing that he had been successful, the prior of St Florian gave him his blessing for the new venture.

Still Bruckner hesitated. There was a final examination on 25th January 1856, before which written applications had to be submitted. Bruckner made no move, but was firmly persuaded and pressed into action. At the same time he was told to remember to dress carefully when meeting influential people and never to appear again 'in your overcoat which was even missing a button, and with a scarf around your neck'. These details sorted out, Bruckner faced three other candidates at the January audition and displayed 'such exceptional ability' that he was appointed. But his agonies of uncertainty were resolved only when he received an assurance that his job at St Florian would be kept open for him in case he felt he wanted to come back. Thus Bruckner, now in his thirty-second year, cautiously embarked on his professional musical career.

Life in Linz was hectic. Bruckner was organist at both the cathedral and the *Pfarrkirche*, he took piano pupils, practised for hours each day at the organ, and became an active member (and shortly afterwards librarian) of the Linz choral society, the *Liedertafel* '*Frohsinn*'. On the other hand, he was released from the monotonous round of teaching duties, had free lodgings with a salary of about 520 florins, and made many friends in the lively town, including Moritz von Mayfeld and his wife, and the brothers Alois and Rudolf Weinwurm. Another friend was the theatre conductor Ignaz Dorn, who introduced him to Liszt's *Faust Symphony*. The organ of the old cathedral in Linz, in its day one of the finest Austrian instruments, still exists as Bruckner knew it. A third manual was added during his years there. Bruckner's favourite organ in the district was at the monastery of Wilhering—a small but delightful one-manual-and-pedals instrument which also still exists. He was again fortunate in his superior, Bishop Franz Josef Rudigier, a genuine lover of music, who became a warm friend and admirer and was perhaps the first person to appreciate and foster the early signs of his creative maturity.

Each day anything up to seven hours was devoted to exercises for Sechter, the tuition being largely carried on by correspondence. After receiving *seventeen* notebooks filled with exercises on one occasion, Sechter wrote back:

> I really must implore you to take more care of yourself and to allow yourself sufficient relaxation. I can assure you that I am fully convinced of your thoroughness and eagerness and I do not want your health to suffer under too great a mental strain. I feel I have to tell you that I have never had a more dedicated pupil.

Bruckner made the journey to Vienna twice a year, during Advent and Lent when the organ was silent in church. He became friendly with Sechter on these visits of six or seven weeks' duration, and spent every day from morning till evening in his teacher's home. At the end of each term he insisted on having a testimonial about his progress. When on 10th July 1858 he sat an examination in harmony, figured bass and organ-playing, Sechter wrote in his testimonial that 'Bruckner shows much versatility in improvisation and in developing a theme and may therefore be counted as one of the finest of organists'. A Viennese critic, Ludwig Speidel, attended Bruckner's organ-playing in the *Piaristenkirche* on this occasion, and wrote an article full of praise in the *Wiener Zeitung*. Step by step Bruckner completed the various stages of Sechter's course, passing elementary counterpoint on 12th August 1859, advanced counterpoint on 3rd April 1860 and canon and fugue on 26th March 1861, thus concluding his theoretical studies and receiving a final glowing testimonial. Sechter was so completely satisfied that he celebrated the occasion by writing a fugue and dedicating it to Bruckner.

Meanwhile Bruckner's mother had died. He was greatly upset by her death and regretted that she had never joined him in Linz as he had frequently urged. In November of the same year, 1860, he was appointed conductor of the *Liedertafel 'Frohsinn'*, which provided a welcome opportunity for more practical music-making after his years of theoretical study, and was also a new stimulus towards composition. After his final examination with Sechter, Bruckner was able to enjoy to the full his activities with the choir. They visited numerous choral festivals; their performances drew much praise and caught the attention of Johann Herbeck in Nürnberg. An influential musician, Herbeck was to become a firm friend of Bruckner and a faithful promoter of his work in the Vienna years. A fine setting of 'Ave Maria' for seven-part chorus was first performed in Linz on May 12th and the occasion marked Bruckner's first concert appearance as a composer. While the choir was in Nürnberg during September, he fell for the charms of yet another young girl, called Olga, a waitress in a restaurant frequented by the choir. One evening the choir decided to play a prank on Bruckner: they persuaded Olga, seductively dressed, to go up to a room where they had left Bruckner alone. Her entrance did not amuse him at all, and he ran from the restaurant, insulted, annoyed and upset, and at once resigned his conductorship of the choir.

Bruckner applied for the conductorship of the *Dommusikverein und Mozarteum* in Salzburg, but as a result of various intrigues the post was awarded elsewhere. He then applied for the diploma of the Vienna Conservatorium, a qualification which would entitle him to teach harmony and counterpoint in schools of music. In October he submitted Sechter's testimonials, some counterpoint exercises and a number of free compositions, and in November he was examined at the organ of the *Piaristenkirche*, Vienna, by Herbeck, Hellmesberger, Sechter, Dessoff and the school supervisor, Becker. It was his greatest examination triumph, and the effect of his improvisation on a long and difficult theme was summed up by Herbeck with the words: 'He should have examined us.' It was an occasion not unlike Walther before the Mastersingers, but Bruckner still had to face his Beckmesser, who was alive and well in Vienna too. Meanwhile another success followed in December, when two works, the Psalm 146 for soloists, chorus and orchestra, and the offertory 'Afferentur regi' for mixed chorus, three trombones and organ, were first performed at Linz.

About this time he met Otto Kitzler, first cellist of the municipal theatre in Linz. The meeting was perfectly timed, for Kitzler, although only in his twenties and a small figure when compared with the renowned Sechter, was able to share with Bruckner his keen interest in contemporary music and his knowledge of orchestration. Bruckner took lessons from the younger man in musical form and orchestration. His early work included analyses of Beethoven sonatas and of works by Mendelssohn and an orchestration of the first movement of Beethoven's *Pathétique* sonata. Kitzler encouraged Bruckner to compose, and in 1862 some choral works (including a cantata for the laying of the foundation stone of the new Linz Cathedral on 1st May), a String Quartet in C minor, a march for military band, another for orchestra (in D minor) and three short orchestral pieces were composed, as well as a number of exercises in piano-sonata writing. These instrumental works were regarded by Bruckner as student exercises and nothing more.

On 13th February 1863 Kitzler unknowingly performed his greatest service to his pupil. He mounted the first Linz performance of Wagner's *Tannhäuser*, and in their lessons he and Bruckner studied the score together, along with Liszt's symphonic poems. Within a year or two Bruckner was to be labelled (and to this day is often confusedly thought to be) a Wagnerian symphonist. This was to bring him a great deal of misery in later years, and was to hamper understanding of his music long after his death. Though the extent of Wagner's influence upon him will be discussed in a later chapter, it is essential to see his early Wagnerian experiences in perspective. Undoubtedly the works of Wagner which he heard in the 1860s had a tremendous effect on him, opening up new concepts of harmony, orchestration and time-scale. Yet he was thirty-eight and his musical foundations were already securely laid: the Baroque composers whom he had sung at St Florian, mastered at the organ and studied with Sechter; the German Gothic tradition; and the early Romantics—Schubert, Weber and Mendelssohn. Furthermore he was no mean contrapuntist, as is shown by accounts of his improvisation and by a work such as the Missa Solennis of 1854, and no stranger to the skills of subtle harmonic effects: many pieces containing 'Wagnerian' harmony date from years before he was spellbound by turning the pages of the score of

Tannhäuser. But Wagner was the catalyst that set these foundations alight and awoke Bruckner's individuality.

In 1862 he applied without success for the post of *Expektant* organist (organist-designate) at the Imperial Court Chapel (the *Hofkapelle*). On Christmas Eve he began an Overture in G minor and completed it on 22nd January This, his first really impressive orchestral essay, was still regarded by the composer as a mere study, as was his somewhat less effective Symphony in F minor, written in three months between February and May 1863. Around this time Kitzler gave performances of Wagner's *The Flying Dutchman* and *Lohengrin*, which Bruckner presumably attended. On 10th July Kitzler declared Bruckner to be a master, and Bruckner commented later that he felt like a watchdog that had at last snapped his chain. Two other works completed this year are important stages in his unfolding: the Psalm 112 with which he felt he had mastered both choral and orchestral composition, and a large-scale work for male chorus and brass band, *Germanenzug*, which he regarded as his first real composition and which was his first work to be published (1865).

In the summer he took a holiday, visiting the Salzkammergut, and in September spent a day or two at the 11th Music Festival in Munich. While there he called on Franz Lachner, a leading conductor and former pupil of Sechter, who had been friendly with Schubert and admired by Beethoven. Lachner (who subsequently joined the anti-Wagner camp) showed interest in the F minor Symphony. Returning to Linz, Bruckner began another symphony, in D minor, which he completed in the spring of 1864. This work was a great leap forward and it immediately preceded his first truly individual large-scale work, written that summer, a Mass, also in D minor. This was also his greatest public triumph to date as a composer. The first performance on 20th November at Linz was received with acclaim and a concert performance followed in December. Bishop Rudigier admitted that he had been unable to pray during the performance owing to the beauty and artistry of the music. But the year had its shadows, some of them cast by unhappy attempts at love. Time and time again Bruckner fell hopelessly in love with girls in their late teens, and the result was always the same. He was liked as a character but was too old to be considered as a husband—he was now forty. Late in the year he wrote to Rudolf Weinwurm threatening to emigrate to Russia or Mexico. (Certain far-away, mysterious lands held a fascination for him—Mexico, Russia or the North Pole.)

In January 1865 he began a Symphony in C minor which had advanced quite far by the spring, when he received an invitation from Wagner himself to attend the first performance of *Tristan und Isolde* in Munich in May. On arrival in Munich he found that the première had been postponed owing to the indisposition of Frau Schnorr (Isolde). So for two weeks he was in Wagner's presence: 'I introduced myself to the Master who proved unusually kind and friendly towards me, seeming to take a liking to me at once. I could not even bring myself to sit down in his presence at first, but he was reassuringly congenial and invited me to join his circle every evening.'

It is interesting to note that in studying *Tristan* Bruckner used a piano score without text—a sign of how unconcerned he was with opera as drama. He showed the beginnings of the C minor symphony to Hans von Bülow, who at thirty-five was more approachable than he later became, and who was enthusiastic; Anton Rubinstein also found the work 'interesting and talented'. He was too afraid to show it to Wagner. He had to go back to Linz before the first night of *Tristan* and was not able to return to Munich until the third performance of the opera. 'Wagner was very glad to see me and thanked me personally for having come again, but I did not dare show him any compositions of mine even then.'

At a June choral competition in Linz his *Germanenzug* was first heard but he was upset at receiving only second prize. This was the occasion of his first meeting with the Viennese critic Eduard Hanslick, who at this time displayed nothing but friendliness, listening to Bruckner improvising at the organ, giving him advice, and presenting him with a signed photograph. Another meeting this year was with Liszt, in Pest, where he heard *St Elizabeth*. He had previously met Berlioz in Vienna at a performance of *La Damnation de Faust*. How Bruckner fared in the company of these sophisticated arch-Romantics is left to our imagination.

Work on the C minor symphony continued into 1866, and his sister 'Nani' came to live with him in Linz, providing him with much needed company. He pursued two girls in the course of the year: Josephine Lang, who was seventeen and who rejected him because of the difference in their ages—which filled him with dismay—and Henriette Reiter, a 'lovely, dear girl' aged eighteen. With Henriette he inquired into all the details of her family position, social standing and financial status so as to approach marriage with her in the most business-like way, but the approach as ever was doomed to failure. He heard Beethoven's Ninth Symphony at this time and completed his own C minor symphony (No. 1, 1866), and in November, the second of his great Mass settings, in E minor, commissioned by Bishop Rudigier. A combination of overwork, fears for the future, anxieties about gaining recognition as an artist and frustrated attempts at love led to severe depression and a total nervous collapse. He was admitted on 8th May 1867 to a sanatorium at Bad Kreuzen, and his letters from there show that this was a time of grave crisis. He spoke of impending madness, threatened suicide and regarded himself as utterly forsaken by the world. He also developed numeromania—an obsessive, neurotic condition which impelled him to count the leaves on trees, grains of sand, the stars, logs in a woodpile and so on. His friend Frau Mayfeld, who was staying at the sanatorium for a water-cure, could not wear one of her dresses as Bruckner started to count the pearls on it whenever he met her. Later in life these symptoms were to recur, and in his scores Bruckner meticulously numbered every bar and added up phrase-groups. Bishop Rudigier sent a priest to look after him. In a letter to Weinwurm of 19th June even the punctuation reveals his excitement and anxiety:

Whatever you think or may have thought—or whatever you may have heard!—! It was not laziness!—It was much more than that!!!—!; it was a condition of utter degeneration and loneliness—total collapse of nerves and exhaustion! I was in the most appalling state; you are the only person to hear of this—please keep quiet about it. In a little while I should have been a victim—lost. Doctor Fadinger of Linz told me that I could by now have been possessed by madness. God be thanked! He has saved me in time. . . . I am not permitted to play anything, or study or work. Only think what a fate! What a wretched man I am! Herbeck sent me the score of my vocal Mass and of the symphony without writing a word. Are they as bad as that? Please find out. Write to me, dear friend!

On 8th August he left the sanatorium quite restored and relaxed. He applied for a lectureship in harmony and counterpoint at Vienna University, and again to the *Hofkapelle* for a position. In the latter application he made the extraordinary suggestion: 'Moreover I could be employed as a secretary and teacher in the principal schools, as I have served as a teacher for fourteen years.' Both applications were rejected, to Bruckner's great disappointment, but Johann Herbeck decided that he should be appointed professor of harmony and counterpoint at the Vienna Conservatorium to succeed Simon Sechter, who had died on 10th September. Meanwhile, on 16th January 1868, Bruckner was reappointed conductor of the *Liedertafel 'Frohsinn'* and from September 1867 until September of the following year wrote his third great Mass, in F minor, which was the last work of his Linz period. A Phrygian 'Pange lingua' and an offertory, 'Inveni David,' also belong to 1868. Bruckner had requested a work from Wagner for the *Liedertafel* centenary concert on

4th April. Not having a suitable original work, Wagner wrote a friendly letter suggesting the last section of his newly completed *Die Meistersinger von Nürnberg*, and so Hans Sachs's famous solo at the end of Act 3, and the final chorus, were first heard in Linz under the baton of Anton Bruckner along with his own *Vaterlandsliebe* (1866).

At Easter he was officially offered Sechter's old post at the Vienna Conservatorium. Just as when he moved from St Florian to Linz, he became anxious, indecisive and afraid. He was dependent on his good salary at Linz and had been promised a pension for his old age. He wrote some pitiful letters including one to Herbeck in which he threatened to 'leave the world', and another to Bülow, requesting his help and that of Wagner to secure him a well-paid court or theatre post at Munich. He made a renewed attempt at obtaining the conductorship of the Salzburg *Dommusikverein* but was merely offered honorary membership.

On 9th May his Symphony in C minor (No. 1) was first performed at Linz under his own baton. Despite an inadequate performance and an inadequate audience (the bridge over the Danube had collapsed the previous day, distracting the populace) the occasion was a success. Mayfeld praised the work in the *Linzer Zeitung* and Hanslick, so far loyal, wrote in the Vienna press: 'There are rumours that Bruckner is to join the staff of the Vienna Conservatorium. If these should be correct, we may well congratulate the institution.' But Bruckner was still disturbed about the idea. Only when Herbeck had succeeded in raising his salary from 600 to 800 florins, when he was also appointed *Expektant* organist at the *Hofkapelle* and when the authorities at Linz promised to keep his job open as a line of retreat, did he move, with his sister 'Nani', in the summer of 1868, to Höhne-Haus, Wöhringerstrasse 41, Vienna.

4 Vienna

When Bruckner arrived in Vienna, it was the heyday of Johann Strauss the younger, and the city was a backcloth of elegant boulevards for a sparkling society and for frivolous gaiety, waltzes and operettas. It was also the home of Brahms, whom most of the musical circles in the city, including the mightiest of the critics, Hanslick, regarded as the heir of Beethoven. The antipode of Brahms was Wagner, and after him Liszt. The two hostile camps were quite irreconcilable. But during his first winter in Vienna, Bruckner attended Hanslick's lectures at Vienna University on the history of music.

Duties at the *Konservatorium der Gesellschaft der Musikfreunde* began on 1st October 1868. Bruckner had an easy, lively method of teaching, with the gift of presenting an academic point in an enjoyable, even amusing way.[1] But he was as strict and severe as Sechter when it came to the standards he expected of his students, and he allowed no free composition during the course. He was certainly one of the greatest composers of the century to apply himself to the teaching of harmony and counterpoint, and no one could have been better equipped for the task. His first pupils included the young virtuoso pianist Wladimir de Pachmann, the future Bruckner interpreter Felix Mottl and, shortly after, Guido Adler. Other pupils of the Vienna years who attained distinction included his future editors Franz Schalk and Ferdinand Löwe, his future biographer August Göllerich,

[1] He called the diminished seventh chord the 'musical Orient Express' because it can take one so quickly to faraway places.

the writers Ernst Decsey and Friedrich Eckstein, the conductors Rudolf Krzyyzanowski, Emil Paur and Arthur Nikisch, the composers Friedrich Klose, Cyrill Hynais, František Marschner, Ernest Schelling and Camillo Horn, and the organist Hans Rott. Rott was a declared favourite of Bruckner's, a fine organist and a friend of Mahler. (He died insane about 1881.) Bruckner soon had another rise in salary and in December 1868 the Ministry of Education awarded him 500 florins for 'the composition of major symphonic works'.

His post at the *Hofkapelle* was an honorary one and in addition to duties as organist he became vice-librarian and second singing-teacher to the choristers. He was not an outstanding success at the *Hofkapelle*, was rarely asked to play on great occasions and found little opportunity to show his skills as an improviser there. It was only in later years that the emperor and his family expressly requested him to play at important private celebrations. In fact Bruckner never excelled as an accompanist of choirs. Liszt complained of his dragging accompaniment at a performance of one of his oratorios. There were some unfavourable criticisms of his organ-playing, although these were more than likely due to musical politics. He was but an average pianist and violinist, he had gained a good deal of experience as a choral singer, he was a competent conductor of choirs, but largely unsuccessful as an orchestral conductor and his performances of his own symphonies suffered because of this.

The close of 1868 saw some rehearsals, under Herbeck, of the F minor Mass, but these were poorly attended, and the first performance of the work did not materialize for three years. In January of the next year Bruckner began revising the D minor symphony and continued this task until September. It became known as 'No. 0' (*Die Nullte*) and, like the early 'study symphony' in F minor, was never included by Bruckner in his official canon of symphonies. (A year before his death he wrote on the score 'Only an attempt—totally invalid', but he bequeathed the work to a museum in Linz.) About this time, Dessoff, the conductor of the Vienna Philharmonic Orchestra, rejected the First Symphony on account of its wildness and daring, and he thought little more of *Die Nullte,* the revision of which was interrupted by an invitation to visit France in April 1869.

Hanslick must take the credit for the choice of Bruckner to take part in a series of recitals on a new organ in the Church of St Epvre, Nancy. At Nancy his playing of Bach and his improvisation made such an impression that he was asked to go on to Paris, where he played on the organ of Notre Dame before a distinguished audience which included Saint-Saëns, Franck, Auber, Gounod and Ambroise Thomas. His Paris improvisations were remembered with admiration in later years. On his way home he stayed in Wels and here another young lady, Karoline Rabl, caught his eye and awoke his longing for marriage.

The triumphs in France were followed on 25th September by a moving première of the Mass in E minor outside Linz Cathedral, and one of his most beautiful motets, 'Locus iste', of this year was first heard in Linz in October. He was made an honorary citizen of Ansfelden and an honorary member of the Linz *Liedertafel.* His next symphonic essay consisted of sketches for a Symphony in B flat major—the only example of a major key used for a symphonic work at this time. But the plan was to give way to work on Symphony No. 2, although the sketches provided material for both this and the Fourth Symphony.

In 1870 Bruckner's sister 'Nani' died, after looking after him for four years. Soon he took a housekeeper, Katharina Kachelmayr ('Frau Kathi'), who stayed with him until his death. She cared for him in a motherly fashion, and although they often squabbled her services were invaluable to him. He was awarded a further grant of 400 florins from the Ministry of Education, and towards the end of the year was appointed teacher of piano, organ and theory at the teacher-training college of St Anna, which raised his salary by 500 florins but gave him less time for creative work. He also took private pupils.

He was selected to represent Austria in a series of six recitals on the new Henry Willis organ at the Royal Albert Hall, London, in August 1871. The English press was more reserved in its enthusiasm than the French, but the result of the Albert Hall appearances was a further five recitals at the Crystal Palace. The *Morning Advertiser* of 1st September spoke of his playing of Bach and Mendelssohn as 'truly excellent . . . leaving nothing to be desired', and went on:

Herr Bruckner excels in his improvisation. You will find great easiness and abundance of ideas, and the ingenious method by which such an idea is carried out is very remarkable. The London public has fully acknowledged Herr Bruckner's perfect execution and may have expressed a hope that this first visit may not be the last. We join in. Bruckner may publish some of his most successful compositions for the benefit and enjoyment of the musical public, who, we are sure, would be very pleased to become better acquainted with the works of this thorough artist.

The highlight of at least one recital was an improvisation 'on English melodies' including *God Save the Queen*. He told Mayfeld in a letter from his hotel in Finsbury Square that he had played at one concert before an audience of 70,000 and had to give encores, and that the conductor, Manns, had asked him to come again and introduce himself as a composer. This came to nothing, and a planned series of recitals in the major towns of England for the following year never materialized. Yet Bruckner frequently longed to return to England, and in moments of trial in Vienna seriously thought of doing so.

A silly scandal awaited him on returning to Vienna. In his rough, straightforward Upper Austrian dialect he had innocently addressed a girl in the college of St Anna in a familiar way ('lieber Schatz') and a great fuss had been made. Bruckner was upset and asked to be relieved of his duties in the female section of the college, which meant losing some of his salary. Characteristically he was not calmed until Hellmesberger, the director of the Conservatorium, supplied him with a testimonial confirming perfect discipline in his classes there. He began his Symphony No. 2 (like the First, in C minor) in October 1871 and revised the F minor Mass for its first performance at the *Augustinerkirche* on 16th June 1872. He conducted himself, and the work was enthusiastically received. Herbeck commented: 'I know only two Masses—this one and Beethoven's Missa Solennis.' Brahms was present and was deeply moved, Hanslick gave it some praise in the *Neue Freie Presse*, and Liszt thought very highly of it.

Work progressed on the Second Symphony, especially when Bruckner found time to make one of his regular visits to a retreat in Upper Austria. He completed it on 11th September 1872 and immediately sent it to Dessoff, who rehearsed it with the Vienna Philharmonic and sent it back with the verdict, 'unplayable'. Despite this, Bruckner pressed on with another symphony, No. 3 in D minor, which occupied him from February until 31st December 1873. Armed with this manuscript and other scores, he set off in the summer for Marienbad and Karlsbad and finally reached Bayreuth in September 1873, where he determined to meet Wagner again. Wagner was busy working at the *Ring* and at first tried to get rid of the persistent intruder. The famous meeting is best described in Bruckner's own words: [1]

I said: 'Master, I have no right to rob you of even five minutes, but I am convinced that the highly acute glance of the Master would only have to see the themes, and the Master would know what to think of it all.' Then the Master said to me, 'Very well then, come along!' And he took me into the drawing room and looked at the Second Symphony. 'Very nice', he said, but none the less it did not seem bold enough for him (at that time the Viennese had made me very timid), and he took the Third (D minor) and with the words, 'Look! Look!

[1] Letter to Hans von Wolzogen, September 1884.

I say! I say!' he went through the entire first part (commenting particularly on the trumpet [1]) and then he said: 'Leave this work here; after lunch [it was then twelve o'clock] I will have another look at it.' I thought, dare I ask him before he says I may? Very shyly and with a pounding heart I then said to the Master: 'Master! there is something in my heart that I lack courage to speak of.' The Master said: 'Out with it! You know how I like you!' Then I presented my petition (that is the intention of dedicating the work to him), but only if the Master was more or less satisfied, as I did not wish to do sacrilege to his most celebrated name. The Master said: 'This evening at five o'clock you are invited to Wahnfried; you will see me then; after I have had a good look at the D minor Symphony we can discuss the matter.'

Afterwards Wagner told him that he accepted the dedication with 'immense pleasure' and they drank beer together and Wagner showed him his grave, whereupon Bruckner knelt and prayed. Overwhelmed with the result of the meeting and feeling the effects of too much beer, Bruckner could not remember on the following day which of the two works Wagner had accepted, so he sent a note to him:

> Symphony in D minor where the trumpet begins the theme?
> Anton Bruckner.

Wagner wrote hastily underneath this:

> Yes! Yes! Best wishes!
> Richard Wagner.

After his Bayreuth visit Bruckner joined the *Akademischer Richard Wagner-Verein* and this, together with his pride at the composer's recognition of him, led to his growing reputation in Vienna as a Wagnerian.

On 26th October he conducted the Vienna Philharmonic in the first performance of Symphony No. 2—a concert arranged by Herbeck who had at length found a willing patron in the person of Prince Johann Liechtenstein. The evening included

[1] Thus Wagner's nickname for Bruckner—the Trumpet.

a much-praised organ improvisation by the composer. Ludwig Speidel wrote most favourably about the work and so on the whole did Hanslick, who took the opportunity, however, to point out its 'Wagnerian' derivation. Afterwards Bruckner wrote to the orchestra offering the dedication of the work. They never replied. The Third Symphony was completed in its first form and contained a number of quotations from Wagner's works. Its writing had given Bruckner much joy. It was also to bring him more pain than any other work and he began a revision of it as early as 1874. Two days elapsed between the completion of the Third Symphony and the first sketches for a Fourth, in E flat major, on 2nd January 1874, and this work was in turn complete by 22nd November.

It was a year of unsuccessful attempts at improving his fortunes. When his post at the college of St Anna was terminated for economic reasons, he applied for a government grant, renewed his 1867 application for a lectureship in the university and tried to find backing for a move to England. All these attempts failed, but the university application has some interest as applications for a music lectureship went to the Dean of the Music Faculty—Eduard Hanslick. Hanslick felt that there was no need for such a post as his own lectures covered the fields of harmony and counterpoint adequately, and he made this clear in his reports to the State authorities. He also made some barbed attacks on Bruckner, who persisted and wrote no fewer than three further applications, each followed by a clear 'No' from Hanslick, who wrote:

In order to be spared the necessity of enlarging on this point I permit myself the request that the honourable committee of professors should give attention to the remarkable style of Bruckner's application.

I find in this application no facts that call for a revision of my previous views respecting this matter. There is, furthermore, no evidence present to show that Herr Bruckner has ever produced striking results as a teacher of composition.

Bruckner was encouraged in these applications by Karl Edler von Stremayr, Minister of Education, and a professor, August Göllerich (father of Bruckner's biographer-to-be), and in December there was even a mention of the affair in a newspaper.

But poor Bruckner was a 'Wagnerian'. Wagner, on a visit to Vienna, ignored a committee of welcome at the station and went up to Bruckner saying: 'When will the symphony be performed?', and then turning to the others: 'Bruckner! He is my man!' Since Bruckner's real interest in the dramatic content of Wagner's music dramas appears to have been nil, this state of affairs is sad to contemplate. It may have been that Wagner was at times condescending to Bruckner (perhaps for diplomatic reasons) and like Liszt may have found his extreme adoration and obsequiousness somewhat fulsome. But a word of praise from Wagner could put right any venom of Hanslick's, and so Bruckner continued to strive to establish his place in Vienna, where all the signs indicated he was swimming against a powerful tide.

5 Awakened mastery

The story of Bruckner's life now becomes the story of his symphonies—a story highlighted by achievements, triumphs and honours and yet darkened by the disappointments and problems that these massive works brought in their wake. Dessoff promised in October 1874 to perform the Third Symphony and shortly after went back on his word with the excuse that the programme was full. In the following year he rehearsed the newly completed Fourth Symphony and returned it with the opinion that only the first movement might merit a performance. And yet Bruckner had no hesitation about embarking on a new symphony, No. 5 in B flat major. In this he was finally to master the new and vast concept of symphonic structure that he had been forging in the Third and Fourth Symphonies. Ironically it was the only one of his eight completed mature symphonies of which he was never to hear a note played.

On 12th January 1875 he wrote to Mayfeld complaining of his difficulties in arranging a performance of the Third Symphony, of his poor financial state and of the dearth of pupils:

You will now realize how serious my situation has become. I would happily settle abroad if only I were assured an existence. Where shall I turn? Nothing could have persuaded me to come to Vienna if I had only had a hint of what was ahead. It would be simple for my enemies to force me out of the Conservatorium. I am really surprised that they have not already done so. . . . My life has been robbed of every joy—through pure malice. How gladly I would return to my old post at Linz! If only I had gone to England then!

He strove once more in August to persuade the Philharmonic to play the Third Symphony but was refused.

Meanwhile he had applied yet again for a university lectureship, and this time, despite Hanslick's opposition, was appointed in an honorary capacity and gave his inaugural lecture on 25th November, while still at work on the Symphony No. 5. Bruckner enjoyed his work at the university with his 'gaudeamuses', as he called his students. His teaching methods have been preserved in books by his pupils, Klose, Eckstein and Schwanzara. His clear, systematic method was to some extent influenced by Sechter's teaching[1] and he never taught 'real' composition or introduced the new, creative thoughts of Liszt or Wagner into his classes. He was an admirable teacher of the fundamental elements of musical construction and he was liked for his individuality and warm personality. Many of his pupils at this time became his future champions and he delighted to spend evenings with groups of them over beer and supper at an inn or restaurant, when the conversation no doubt ranged over new and progressive ideas in music. His young adherents at this time included a teenage boy, Gustav Mahler, who became a friend and later interpreter, although he never studied with him.

In 1876 the three great Masses were all slightly revised and the Fifth Symphony was completed in May. The Second Symphony had received another performance in February with Bruckner conducting. This concert had also been arranged by Herbeck but he pressed Bruckner into making a number of drastic cuts, and this set an unfortunate precedent for the revisions of later years. The work had a mixed reception and while the audience applauded vigorously, one critic called Bruckner 'a fool and a half', and Hanslick wrote a hostile review criticizing the 'lack

[1] e.g., the 'interdominant' theory. In progressions of triads with no common note, an imaginary, intermediate root harmony is postulated, so D-E is D-B-E. Schoenberg stressed this idea in his teaching of step-wise progressions.

of form'. This may be the reason for further revisions of the Second Symphony in 1877. During these years he regularly visited Upper Austria in the summer, often staying at St Florian, and in August 1876 he attended the first performance of the *Ring* at Bayreuth and renewed his friendship with Wagner.

In January 1877 he applied unsuccessfully for the post of conductor at the church *am Hof*. He moved during the year to a rent-free fourth-floor flat at Hessgasse 7, in the house of an admirer, Dr Anton Özelt-Newin, whom he had met on a visit to Klosterneuburg, and he stayed at this address until 1895. In this spacious apartment, which had a fine view of the city, he lived in simplicity. His bedroom contained only an English brass bed, presented by his pupils ('my luxury'), some portraits and a bust of himself. The other, blue-walled room contained his piano, harmonium, armchair, worktable and chest of drawers. In the hall he made a collection of laurel wreaths awarded to him, and stacks of music and manuscript paper lay all around.

The sorry history of the Third Symphony continued. During 1876–7 it was again revised and the Wagner quotations (from *Tristan* and *Die Walküre*) were removed. He completed the revision on 28th April 1877. Herbeck planned to conduct a performance of it, but died suddenly on 28th October. August Göllerich and his son (Bruckner's pupil) arranged for the performance to go on, however, on 16th December, but Bruckner had to conduct. Before the concert he wrote to a sympathetic critic in Berlin, Wilhelm Tappert:

Our Philharmonic is absolutely antagonistic to the 'New Order' in music. I shall never submit any of my works to them again, for they have rejected my offerings repeatedly. How Richter can remain on the best terms with Wagner's bitterest opponents is truly amazing to me. Alas, I too have come to know him as the arch-liar he is. Only recently have many of Wagner's statements become clear to me. I implore you not to be turned against me by the malicious statements that are made about me.

The première of Symphony No. 3 came at the end of a long programme and was an almost unmitigated disaster, partly due to the fact that its scale was beyond Bruckner's conducting ability. The audience left the hall in growing numbers and when the last note sounded, and the orchestra had fled the platform, 'that fraction of the public which had remained to the end consoled him for the flight of the rest', to put it in Hanslick's words. Hanslick imagined the work as 'a vision of Beethoven's Ninth becoming friendly with Wagner's Valkyries and finishing up trampled under their hooves'. Bruckner was in a state of shattered emotion and refused to listen to the consolations of his faithful students. Then, amazingly, Theodor Rättig, a publisher, who had been to rehearsals of the work and had witnessed the *débâcle*, went to him and offered to publish the symphony. So, in 1878, a symphony of his was published with parts, and in a piano-duet reduction prepared by Mahler and Krzyzanowsky. But the dark day of 16th December affected Bruckner to the extent that almost no composition followed for a year; he further revised the Third Symphony, thoroughly revised the Fourth, touched up the Fifth, and allowed the Third to be published in a cut form. The only work of 1878 of lasting merit was a motet, 'Tota pulchra es Maria', one of his best small liturgical works, dedicated to Bishop Rudigier on his silver jubilee.

Bruckner was now appointed a full member of the *Hofkapelle* with an annual salary of 800 florins. Also in 1878 a fine organ was built by Mauracher at the Benedictine monastery of Kremsmünster. Bruckner was no stranger there, but this instrument and the devoted friendship of Fr. Otto Loidol drew him to Kremsmünster more and more in the later years. The monastery had had associations with Haydn, Mozart and Schubert, and its distinguished library was particularly noted for motets of the early seventeenth century. In December Bruckner began his only mature work of chamber music, a String Quintet in F major. Joseph Hellmesberger had asked him for a quartet, but

Bruckner preferred the richer possibilities of quintet writing. The work was finished on 12th July 1879, shortly after the revision of the Fourth Symphony was complete; and in the same year appeared two motets, 'Christus factus est' and 'Os justi', the latter set in the Lydian mode. Hellmesberger found the scherzo of the Quintet 'too difficult' and this movement was replaced by an Intermezzo (completed in December), although in the end the scherzo was retained.

The lessons in string-writing gained in the Quintet benefited the Symphony No. 6 in A major, begun on 24th September. But work on this was interrupted in 1880 by a further revision of the Fourth Symphony, including the writing of a new and dramatic finale. Bruckner applied for the conductorship of the *Wiener Männergesangverein*, but his standing in Vienna was not yet impressive enough for him to be considered even for this. On 6th June Hellmesberger (who so far had not dared perform the Quintet) mounted a performance of the D minor Mass in Vienna. Then Bruckner took a holiday visiting St Florian, the passion play at Oberammergau, Munich and finally Switzerland, where he played organs in Geneva, Freiburg, Berne, Zürich and Lucerne. At Oberammergau he was attracted to one of the 'daughters of Jerusalem', the seventeen-year-old Marie Bartl. He met her at the stage door, was introduced to her family and corresponded with her for about a year. Then she stopped writing.

On returning to Vienna *via* St Florian, Bruckner suffered from an ailment in the feet and legs which troubled him considerably in after years. He settled down to serious work on the Sixth Symphony, and received, after many applications, the consent of the university for a payment of 800 florins for his academic work. In February 1881 Symphony No. 4 was first performed, under Richter. At a rehearsal for this concert occurred the famous and rather touching incident when the overjoyed Bruckner came up to Richter, pressed a small tip into his hand

and said, 'Take this and drink my health with a glass of beer.' Richter wore the coin on his watch chain ever after. The performance was a victory for Bruckner and even the most unfriendly sections of the press gave him credit. The *Neue Freie Presse* spoke of 'an unusual success'. In May he began the first draft of a *Te Deum*, on 3rd September the Sixth Symphony was completed, and in less than three weeks the Seventh Symphony in E major was under way. Bruckner related that the first subject was given to him in a dream by Ignaz Dorn.

Still Hellmesberger was too nervous to perform the Quintet, to Bruckner's disappointment. But Franz Schalk and some other disciples gave a performance of it (without the finale) at a private concert of the *Akademischer Richard Wagner-Verein* in December 1881. The Masses in D minor and E minor were now revised for the last time, the F minor Mass was heard at the *Hofkapelle* and an infatuation with a young girl with a fine contralto voice brought forth a setting of the 'Ave Maria'.

In July he visited Bayreuth for the first performance of *Parsifal*. It was his last meeting with his beloved master and he described it later to Hans von Wolzogen of Bayreuth:

> In 1882, when he was already suffering from severe illness, he once took my hand, saying: 'Don't worry. I myself will perform the symphony and all of your works.' Moved, I could only exclaim: 'Oh, Master!' Then he asked: 'Have you heard *Parsifal*? How do you like it?' And then while he still held my hand, I knelt before him and pressing it to my lips, said: 'Oh Master, I worship you!' Then he said: 'Be calm—Bruckner. Goodnight!!!' These were the Master's last words to me. On the following day he sat behind me at the *Parsifal* performance and I was scolded for applauding too loudly. Herr Baron, please take great care of all this! My most cherished testament!!!—Until yonder, above!!!

Returning through his familiar Upper Austria, he worked earnestly at Symphony No. 7. A mysterious 'Englishman' appeared in this year and extorted a sum of money from him, having raised his hopes for a Cambridge doctorate. Bruckner heard the Sixth Symphony under Jahn in rehearsal, but only the middle two movements reached the public ear on 11th February 1883. A pupil of Bruckner's, Lamberg, reported that while Brahms joined in the colossal ovation, 'Hanslick sat there, frigid and immobile, like a sphinx.' The Quintet had two performances that year. On 13th February, as Bruckner was completing the *Adagio* of his Seventh Symphony, Wagner died in Venice. The closing pages of the movement are Bruckner's tribute to his memory. In August he journeyed to Bayreuth to visit Wagner's grave and at St Florian, on 5th September, he completed the symphony which was soon to alter his fame and fortunes.

6 Growing fame, illness and death

The major choral work of Bruckner's Vienna period, his *Te Deum*, was written in its final form between 28th September 1883 and 7th March 1884. It is in many ways a summation of the man: his mastery of choral writing, his individuality in symphonic integration, and above all the intensity of his religious fervour.

The Quintet had several performances and was also published during 1884. On the whole it drew praise from the critics, including the Brahmans, but one critic, while praising the Quintet itself, saw fit to call Bruckner

> the greatest living musical peril, a sort of tonal anti-Christ. The violent nature of the man is not written in his face, for his expression indicates at most the small soul of an every-day *Kapellmeister*. Yet he composes nothing but high treason, revolution and murder. His work is absolutely devoid of art or reason. . . . His music has the fragrance of heavenly roses, but it is poisonous with the sulphurs of hell.

As well as completing two motets in this year, the 'greatest living musical peril' began his greatest symphony, No. 8 in C minor. He paid a visit to Prague, and on his return met Liszt, to whom he offered the dedication of the Second Symphony. Liszt formally accepted, but left his hotel in a hurry, forgetting to take the score with him. When Bruckner learned this he was hurt and withdrew the dedication. During the year he met Hugo Wolf, at that time critic of the *Wiener Salonblatt*, who immediately became an ardent if not vehement protagonist for him. After a summer visiting Bayreuth, Munich, Kremsmünster and St Florian, he celebrated his sixtieth birthday in Vöcklabruck with his sister Rosalie and the town band honoured the occasion publicly. While there he worked on the Eighth Symphony and took a fancy to a young village girl to whom he brought some flowers each day. She was replaced in his heart, however, in the following spring by another teenager, Marie Denmar.

The première of the Seventh Symphony unlocked a new door in Bruckner's path, and he strode on accompanied by a growing momentum of public acclaim. The performance on 30th December was given in Leipzig by the Gewandhaus Orchestra under Nikisch, and it established his reputation not only in Germany but also internationally. A Leipzig critic wrote:

> One could see from the trembling of his lips and the sparkling moisture in his eyes how difficult it was for the old gentleman to suppress the deep emotion that he felt. His homely, honest countenance beamed with a warm inner happiness such as can appear only on the face of one who is too good-hearted to give way to bitterness even under the weight of most crushing circumstances. Having heard his music, and now seeing him in person, we asked ourselves in amazement, 'How is it possible that he could remain so long unknown to us?'

Herman Levi performed the work in March 1885, again with marked success, and it was also heard during that year in Dresden, Frankfurt, Utrecht, New York and twice in The Hague. Liszt heard the Adagio in Karlsruhe and was thereafter to work tirelessly to further Bruckner's name. Not long before his death Liszt was personally responsible for arranging a concert including the Quintet and the first and third movements of the Fourth Symphony in Sondershausen—a noble gesture from an artist whose own works were rarely heard and subject to marked animosity. The Vienna Philharmonic considered a performance of the Seventh Symphony, but Bruckner begged them not to proceed for fear that Hanslick and the Vienna press might destroy the advantage he had gained abroad. But Gutmann published the work for a fee of 1,000 florins, and King Ludwig II of Bavaria honoured Bruckner by accepting the dedication.

During 1885 he laboured at the Eighth Symphony, wrote two exquisite motets 'Ecce sacerdos' and 'Virga Jesse floruit' and con-conducted a première of the *Te Deum* in Vienna with two pianos substituted for orchestra. Two notable organ improvisations were also given. On 28th August, the feast of St Augustine, patron saint of St Florian, Bruckner gave a mighty rendering of themes from *Götterdämmerung* and from his sketched Eighth Symphony in the *Stiftkirche*: and on the feast of St Leopold, patron saint of Austria, gave a rousing improvisation on the *Kaiserlied* at Klosterneuburg. The emperor was present on the second of these occasions: as he entered to the sound of the organ he was reported to have stood still for a moment, then looked upwards and murmured, 'Ah, Bruckner!' The same year saw a performance by Hellmesberger of the Quintet in Vienna, and of the E minor Mass in Linz. But persistent ailments began to trouble Bruckner, and a form of dropsy set in. These symptoms hampered his busy life, but they did not become acute until his last few years.

Though he applied unsuccessfully for a doctorate to the Universities of Philadelphia and Cincinnati, honours did come. He was decorated by the emperor with the Order of Franz-Josef in June 1886, received by him personally and given a grant of 300 florins from the Imperial purse. He sat for portraits, and Fritz von Uhde honoured him in a way that moved him deeply, by using him as a model for one of the disciples in his painting of the 'Last Supper'. Performances occurred in growing numbers, Symphony No. 3 at Linz and The Hague, No. 4 at Sondershausen, and No. 7 at Graz, Hamburg, Cologne, Amsterdam, New York, Boston and Chicago (in 1886); and in the next year No. 7 was heard in Berlin, Cologne, Budapest, twice in Dresden and twice in London. The *Te Deum* performance was another victory

(Vienna, 10th January 1886) and even Hanslick made some concessions.

However, the Vienna première of the Seventh Symphony was to justify Bruckner's nervousness about the critical reaction. While the performance under Richter (in March 1886) filled the audience with enthusiasm and secured a great ovation for the composer, Hanslick called the work 'unnatural, bombastic, sickly and decadent'. Brahms's official biographer, Kalbeck, said: 'It comes from the Nibelungen and goes to the devil', and Hanslick's mouthpiece Dompke declared that 'Bruckner writes like a drunkard'.

Bruckner visited Prague to play on a new organ and journeyed to Bayreuth in August. Liszt had just died, and Cosima Wagner invited him to take part in her father's funeral. He marked the occasion with a towering improvisation at the organ on themes from *Parsifal*.

Work on the Eighth Symphony continued until 1887, a year that also saw the publication of the *Te Deum* (financed by his pupil Friedrich Eckstein); a number of his smaller sacred works also appearing in print in these years. On 4th September he wrote to Hermann Levi: 'Hallelujah! At long last the Eighth is finished and my artistic father must be the first to know about it. . . . May it find grace!' Levi was a staunch champion of Bruckner, but he could not follow or comprehend this, the longest and most solemn of Bruckner's symphonic canvases. Not wishing to hurt Bruckner directly, he sent news of his failure to appreciate the work *via* Joseph Schalk. The viciousness of Hanslick's attacks, the fiasco of the première of the Third Symphony and the nervous collapse of his Linz years were nothing in comparison to the effect this information had on Bruckner. It marked the greatest setback of his creative career. He was in despair, many of his symptoms of neurosis reappeared, and he thought of suicide. The practical result of the rejection was the beginning of his most intensive and largely disastrous period of revisions and the result of this in turn was that he never completed another symphony. Robert Simpson has pointed out that but for these years of altering and rewriting, he would probably have finished his Ninth Symphony (sketches for which date from the month of Levi's rejection) and might have begun a Tenth.

The revision of the Eighth Symphony began in October 1887 and was not complete until 10th March 1890. Bruckner's life was still full of teaching duties and he allowed himself to be aided in his task of revision by his pupils.[1] His own creative judgment was thus influenced by the opinions of these well-meaning friends, and countless alterations and small details that would never have survived his critical eye under ordinary conditions found their way into the pages of these revisions. This is particularly true in the case of the first published versions of his symphonies, all of which are to a greater or lesser extent spurious. A completely new version of the Third Symphony was worked out during the revision of the Eighth. Some years earlier Bruckner had been persuaded to revise and shorten the Third Symphony and had in fact begun this task, asking the publisher to re-engrave fifty-two pages of the score. Mahler then persuaded him that the revision was superfluous and the plates were scrapped, but now the revising mania could not be checked. Two days after the Eighth was completed a new version of the First Symphony was begun and was in turn completed in April 1891. The F minor Mass was revised from 1890 to 1893.

In 1889 the Fourth Symphony was published as a result of an appeal for finances by Levi,[2] and in the next year the Third Symphony appeared in print, with expenses defrayed by the emperor. Also in 1889 the first payment of an annual grant from a group of Austrian industrialists was made to Bruckner and he was created an honorary member of the *Richard-Wagner-Verein*.

[1] For details see Chapter 9.

[2] Bruckner wrote to the publisher Gutmann requesting that not a note of the parts be altered. His request was ignored.

In the autumn a meeting with Brahms was arranged by friends of the two composers in order to bring the two men closer together. This aim was never realized, but although the meeting at a Viennese restaurant started coldly and formally, the ice was broken when they discovered that they shared an enthusiasm for traditional Austrian dishes. They spent a convivial evening over smoked ham and dumplings but never entered into any debate about music. Although Bruckner had written in February 1885 complaining of Brahms's 'almost insulting behaviour' towards him, it seems that Brahms, who was a master of impoliteness when he chose to be rude, always greeted Bruckner with respect and civility. He never indulged in the public displays of vitriol that Hanslick regarded as his pious duty. In private, Brahms called Bruckner's symphonies 'symphonic boa-constrictors' and 'a swindle that will be forgotten in a few years'. Bruckner in turn said he preferred a Johann Strauss waltz to a Brahms symphony. Strauss returned the compliment, incidentally, and sent a telegram to Bruckner after the first performance of the Seventh Symphony: 'I am deeply moved. It was one of the strongest impressions in my life.'

In the spring of 1890 Bruckner suffered from chronic catarrh of the larynx and his nervous condition further deteriorated. In the autumn he was relieved of his duties as organ professor at the Conservatorium and in December wrote the only work of the entire 1887–91 revision period, a small male-voice chorus, *Träumen und Wachen*. On 21st December the new version of the Third Symphony was heard in Vienna under Richter and received a great ovation.

The year 1891 (the year of Bruckner's retirement from the Conservatorium) saw several triumphs. An ovation almost unprecedented in Berlin musical annals greeted him at a performance of the *Te Deum*, conducted by Siegfried Ochs, in May. While there he met a hotel chambermaid, Ida Buhz, who actually offered to marry him. Meetings with her family (both then and in 1894) ensued, but in 1895 he turned down the idea of a betrothal when it became clear that she would not change her Lutheran faith to become a Catholic. He visited Bayreuth in August for the first Festspielhaus performance of *Tannhäuser*, and at the Mozart festival at Salzburg offered to marry the young Minna Reischl, but her parents opposed the match, although a lively correspondence continued until his death. On 30th October the Upper Austrian Diet voted him an honorary stipend of 400 florins, and on 7th November he received the honour that meant most of all to him—an honorary Ph.D. of the University of Vienna, the first time the award had been made to a musician. Bruckner was so moved at the ceremony that he was unable to reply coherently, ending his confused speech: 'I cannot find words to thank you as I wish, but if there was an organ here I could tell you.' At a gala reception for 3,000 people a month later, in his honour, Dr Adolf Exner spoke the words: 'I, Rector Magnificus of the University of Vienna, bow humbly before the former assistant teacher of Windhaag.'

13th December saw the première of the Symphony No. 1 in its new version, under Richter, and in the following year Psalm 150, in the exultant vein of the *Te Deum*, was written and performed, as were a secular piece, *Das deutsche Lied*, and the last of his motets, 'Vexilla regis'. Bruckner's last visit to Bayreuth was in August 1892, when he prayed daily at Wagner's grave. In the confusion of his arrival, he lost his sketches for the Ninth Symphony, but after some anxious hours they were found at the police station and work continued. On 11th December the Eighth Symphony, dedicated to the emperor, was heard in Vienna under Richter, and was published with the emperor's help, along with the Mass in D minor (with the help of an industrialist, Theodor Haemmerle), the Second Symphony and Psalm 150. The Eighth Symphony was hailed by audience and critics alike as a great success, with the lonely exception of Hanslick, who wrote of its 'dream-disturbed, cat's misery style'.

Liver and stomach complaints necessitated dieting, which Bruckner hated. In 1893 he was confined to bed for a spell, seriously ill. He wrote to his official biographer, Göllerich, on 10th March: 'I feel totally deserted. Nobody comes to see me, or at least only extremely rarely. The *Wagner-Verein* is everything for them.'

He certainly suffered from loneliness in his last years, yet performances were occurring on a wider and more frequent scale and he still received honours such as honorary membership of the *Gesellschaft der Musikfreunde.* The First Symphony was published in 1893, the F minor Mass in 1894, the Fifth Symphony in 1895 and the E minor Mass in 1896. In 1893 he wrote his last completed work, *Helgoland*, for male chorus and orchestra.

At a performance of the F minor Mass in Vienna in 1893 Brahms applauded so warmly that Bruckner went up to his box to thank him for the gesture. Bruckner made his will, in which he bequeathed the original scores of all his important works, containing his true intentions, to the Hofbibliothek in Vienna (now the Österreichisches Nationalbibliothek), 'for later times' as he frequently and significantly remarked. His brother Ignaz and sister Rosalie were named as his heirs. Owing to illness his university lectures were now sporadic and in November 1894 he resigned from the university, thus losing his valued contact with the young. In January of that year he had travelled to Berlin with Hugo Wolf for performances of the *Te Deum* and Seventh Symphony. Wolf's choruses *Der Feuerreiter* and *Elfenlied* were played at one concert which included the première of a work for chorus and orchestra by Eugen d'Albert. But in April Bruckner was too ill to attend the first performance of his Fifth Symphony under Franz Schalk. This performance was of Schalk's own version, a gross perversion of the dying composer's original intentions.

Bruckner spent his seventieth birthday in Steyr. He received telegrams of congratulation from all over the world, many honorary memberships and the freedom of the city of Linz. By the end of November the first three movements of the Ninth Symphony were complete, and he pressed ahead with his most ambitious finale. His health was now very unsteady and his mind often wandered so far that he was incapable of rational conversation. But to the end he had moments of perfect clarity and never lost interest in completing his symphony, which, as he told his doctor, was to be dedicated 'to the King of Kings, our Lord, and I hope that He will grant me enough time to complete it'. He was unable to climb the stairs to his flat and the Emperor put a gate-keeper's lodge at the Schloss Belvedere at his disposal in July 1895.

On 12th January 1896 he attended his last concert—a performance of the *Te Deum* that had been suggested by none other than Johannes Brahms. He was so ill that he had to be carried into the concert hall to hear a programme that included Wagner's *Das Liebesmahl der Apostel* and a new, very advanced symphonic poem, *Till Eulenspiegel*, by Richard Strauss.

The last weeks were clouded by a return of Bruckner's pathological obsessions and there was a hint in his speech of religious mania. Hugo Wolf and Franz Schalk visited him. On Sunday 11th October 1896 he worked on the finale of the Ninth Symphony and in the early afternoon took a walk in the lovely public garden that surrounded the house. Very quietly and without any alarming signs he died on his return. Three days later the *Karlskirche* was thronged by those who came to pay their last respects, and the Adagio of the Seventh Symphony in an arrangement for wind band by Löwe was played. However, two important figures of Bruckner's Vienna years did not enter the church. Hugo Wolf had no ticket and was turned away, and Brahms arrived late, stood at the door, muttered what was thought to be, 'Never mind. Soon my coffin', and left. Bruckner's remains were taken to St Florian, as he had wished, and laid in a splendid sarcophagus exactly beneath the great organ of the *Stiftkirche*.

One of many remarks attributed to him was his reply prepared for the day when his beloved God would call him to account for the use he had made of his earthly talents: 'I will present to him the score of my *Te Deum*, and he will judge me mercifully.'

7 Bruckner's character

Bruckner was outwardly a simple man. His music is far from simple. His psychology is not simple to explain. The word 'simple' has too often become a tag attached to him and it is unsatisfactory. It could imply that he was foolish, half-witted, credulous, inexperienced, insignificant and silly. He was not. He was humble, straightforward, uncomplicated, unpretentious and unsophisticated in outward manner, and it is in this sense, and this sense only, that he can be described as a simple man. He was warm-hearted and childlike, but his proverbial naïvety should not be confused with a lack of intelligence. His rural background was evident all through his life, yet his great-great-grandfather was the last of his ancestors that can truly be called a peasant. City life never really suited him, and the little countryman, habitually dressed in a somewhat bulky black suit and wide-brimmed black hat, was in sharp contrast to the style and elegance of fashionable Vienna. He never lost his native accent and in his speech was capable at times of rustic bluntness.

Many years of his life were spent in subordinate positions and this undoubtedly affected his social behaviour. His letters are straightforward, and his grammar, style and handwriting display an educated mind. Yet his many written applications abound with phrases of respect and devotion that border on the obsequious. This was his natural mode of expression, not a deliberately servile attitude but one that originated in the moulding of his character in the years before the social uprisings of 1848. Social forms, customs and usages of the *Vormärz* period were deeply implanted in his mind, and in 1848 itself he was sheltered at St Florian. His thoughts were in another world and political events did not touch him in the way they did other composers. Furthermore his emergence from this quiet background at an age at which most other composers had made their mark may explain the modest, subservient and often flowery terms of address he used. He took little interest in the contemporary world, and he was not a 'literary' man in any sense. His library contained at his death only books on music and religion, and two other volumes: one on the Mexican war, and the other on a North Pole expedition. The only occasion on which he considered writing an opera was in 1893, when he studied a libretto by Gertrud Bollë-Hellmund called *Astra* (based on a novel, *Die Toteninsel,* by Richard Voss). He admired the style of this for the significant reasons that it was '*à la Lohengrin*, romantic, full of the mystery of religion, and entirely free from all that is impure'.

In a century when many of the great composers were noted for their artistic letter-writing, and when literature and music were united by strong bonds, Bruckner's lack of literary interest is even more striking. But it does not reflect a lack of education or academic ability. He had distinguished himself in all the examinations for his teaching qualifications and later studied Latin, physics and law. Fuchs at Windhaag had criticized him for introducing a controversial and forbidden subject in his classes in those pre-1848 years—the elements of Copernican theory. He had a great interest in medical matters and delighted in questioning medical colleagues at the university. Indeed the university circles in which he mixed would not have tolerated him long if he had displayed an untrained mind.

Another result of his youthful environment was his conservative attitude to life. He unquestioningly accepted authority and a social structure of clear class-distinction. His personal life and surroundings were orderly, and he would never have dreamed of flouting convention. Yet he was no prude, and there are many accounts by his pupils of convivial evenings spent in the company of the kindly old man, who had a warm sense of humour and was a lively conversationalist, especially when music was the topic. He was a keen dancer and always attended many balls during the carnival period, until well into his fifties. He had a large appetite for traditional Austrian cooking and enjoyed beer and good wine, but never apparently drank to excess.

Money matters always worried him a great deal but, although he was never rich, he never suffered poverty. He was always careful to see that his finances were secure and was anxious to be insured and certain of an old-age pension. This explains the continual applications for better-paid posts that he made from his St Florian days until the 1880s. He received only one publisher's fee in his life—a mere 50 florins for the *Te Deum*. Lack of performances seems to have caused him unwarranted anxiety. Every one of his mature works (except the Ninth Symphony) was performed in his lifetime, some of them many times, for example 30 performances of the *Te Deum*, 23 of the String Quintet, 32 of the Seventh Symphony and 24 of the Third Symphony. This was not a record to become depressed about, but the hostility of the critics and his feeling of financial insecurity led him to complain loud and long about the insignificance of public recognition given to him.

In discussing his uncertainty and lack of self-confidence, a careful distinction must be made between personal matters and musical matters. He did not lack self-assurance as a composer, and this is borne out by the fact that each new symphony was written before he had heard a performance of the previous one (with the exception of No. 2), and by the short gaps between the completion of one and the beginning of the next, for example two days between Nos. 3 and 4, two months between Nos. 4 and 5, less than three weeks between Nos. 6 and 7, and hardly any gap between the first version of the Eighth and the first sketch for the Ninth. This remarkable display of self-assertion broke down only under extreme pressure (for example after the first performance of the Third Symphony and after Levi's rejection of the Eighth). Nor does lack of self-confidence account for the feverish revising of the last years. It is clear that his work would not have been heard or published to any comparable extent had he not agreed to these new revisions. It was a weak and regrettable action, but quite understandable and expedient for an artist faced with silence. Bruckner had an utter conviction that what he wrote was what he wanted, and carefully preserved his original scores for future generations. The revisions were made under great pressure and also from an urge for perfection, though at a time when his mental condition reduced him to nervous fussiness.

Worldly matters were different, however. He undoubtedly went into more than one panic of uncertainty during his life. With each step in his career he needed the reassurance of friends and patrons that all would be well, otherwise he became confused, indecisive and incapable of going on. He needed the firmest of ground to tread on, and became obsessed with the collection of testimonials and certificates without which he would have been afraid to proceed in the musical battlefield of Vienna. His long period of study was not the result of a pathological inferiority complex, as has been suggested, but was a necessary stage in his development—an inner compulsion to explore the very essence of music and master every intricacy with infinite patience, without which process his originality might never have been achieved.

It is not necessary to look for historical evidence of Bruckner's belief in himself as a composer. The proof that he knew where he was going, that he discovered his aesthetic and thoroughly mastered it, is in the music itself. And so the strange dichotomy of artist and man reveals itself: Bruckner the man who never lost his Upper Austrian cautiousness, and Bruckner the composer who forged and perfected a conception that was the most significant symphonic step since Beethoven. The facts would suggest that some powerful psychological elements link the provincial organist and the potent symphonic force. A clue may be found in a closer look at his symptoms of nervous disorder, and at his life-long, intense religious fervour.

He frequently oscillated between moods of buoyant optimism and states of depression and despair. The latter were partly the result of distressing professional or emotional experiences, partly inherited (his mother was given to fits of depression), and partly unaccountable, as they occurred even at times of professional success. This temperament, already subject to severe fits of melancholy, was aggravated by a nagging feeling of neglect in the city of the railing Hanslick and the successful Brahms. His three most serious periods of nervous breakdown, which brought him near to insanity, were in 1867, 1887–91 and in the last two years of his life. But for the consolation of his religion and his creative outlet he might well have succumbed to his inner conflicts and obsessions and ended his days in an asylum. Conversely, it may be postulated that but for his inner conflicts he might never have composed.

Manias and obsessions were not confined to periods of crisis. His numeromania is reflected in his scores, both in the meticulous numbering of bars and phrase periods and in obsessive and frenzied repetitions of motifs.[1] He kept a careful list of the number of prayers he said each day, and the number of times he repeated a particular prayer. He also recorded in his diary the number of dances he had with particular girls at a ball. He counted statues during walks in a park and would start all over again if he thought one had been missed. He was obsessed with the need to discover the numbers, characteristics and substance of inanimate objects, such as the ornamental tops of the municipal towers in Vienna. He had an almost macabre interest in death, or more

[1] Schumann had a similar obsession with certain rhythmic constructions.

Bruckner in 1854

Linz

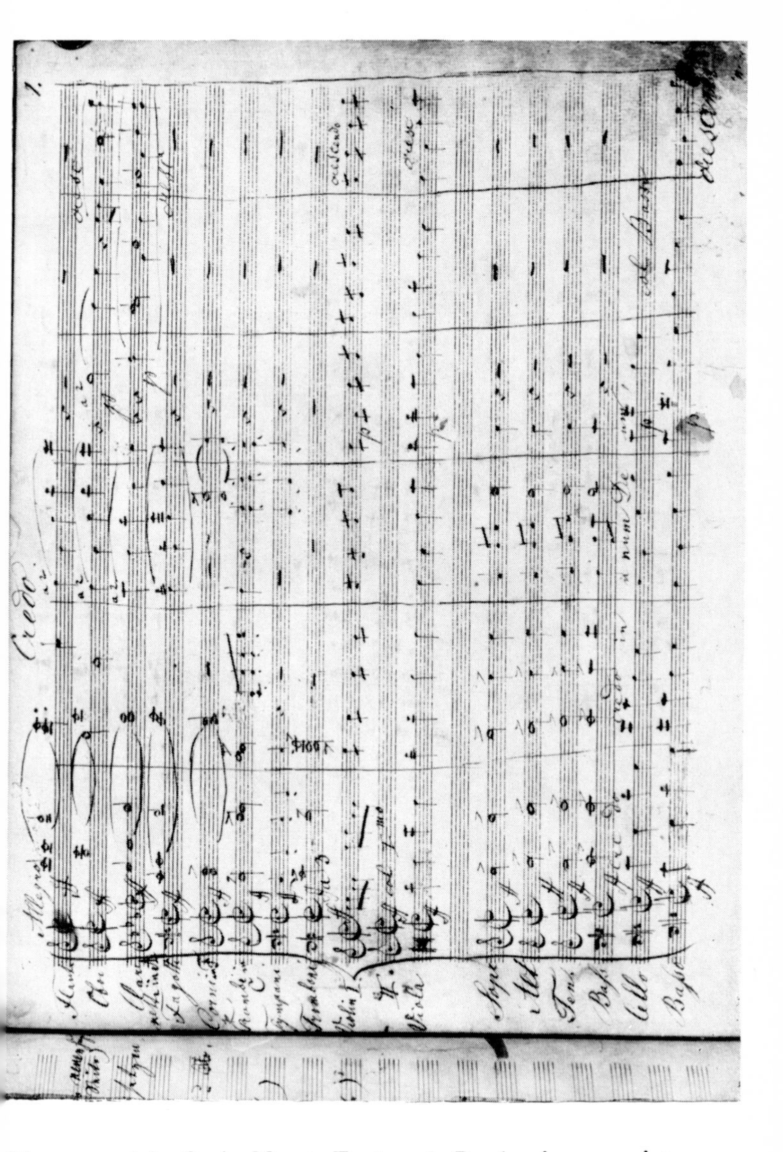

First page of the Credo, Mass in F minor, in Bruckner's manuscript

St Florian: the Collegiate Church

Bruckner about 1890

Bruckner at his Bösendorfer about 1894

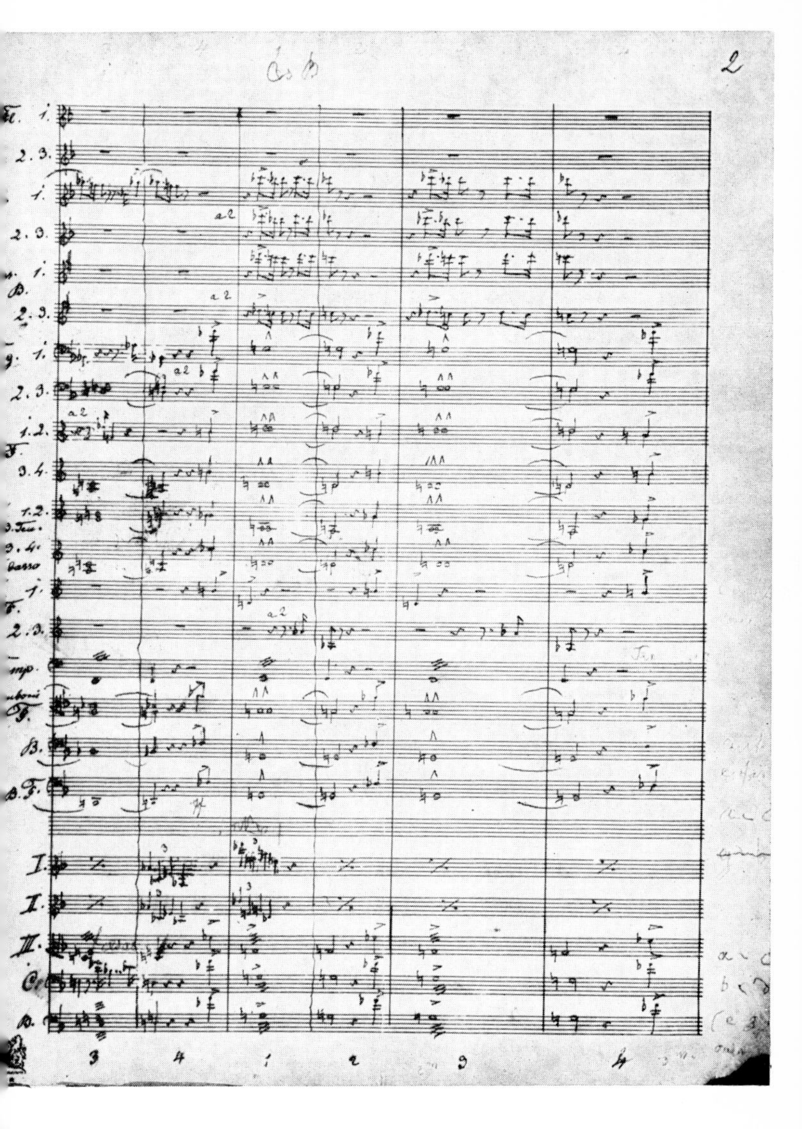

ne finale of Symphony No. 9: a page from the sketch

accurately, in corpses. When Beethoven and Schubert were re-interred in a new burial place, he lost the glass from his pince-nez in his eagerness to catch a glimpse of the remains. He is said to have hurried to the mortuary after a disastrous theatre fire in 1881 to examine the victims' charred bodies, and earlier he had repeatedly requested the Hörsching church authorities to let him have Weiss's skull. In 1868 he wrote to Weinwurm after the assassination of the Emperor Maximilian in Mexico (a country in which he took an intense interest, matched only by the fascination of the severe hardships suffered in a North Pole expedition):

Even during my illness this was the only thing dear to my heart: Mexico and Maximilian. At all costs I want to see the body of Maximilian. Please, Weinwurm, send someone trustworthy to the palace, or even better make enquiries at the office of the *Oberhofmeister* whether it will be possible to view Maximilian's body, i.e. in an open coffin, or under glass, or whether only the closed coffin will be visible. Then please inform me by telegram so that I do not come too late. I ask you most urgently for this information.

His will contained precise details for the disposal of his remains, and it seems fitting that his sarcophagus lies in the crypt of St Florian surrounded by piles of skulls and bones of long-departed brothers of the foundation.

His relations with women, or rather with a succession of young girls, were unsuccessful and unhappy, but do not appear to have seriously disturbed his life or work, although he permanently longed for the security of marriage. In his diary he recorded the names of all the girls who had attracted him, and on his holiday in 1880 the list becomes quite long. He was rejected with unfailing frequency and yet he was never daunted. He wrote in a letter of November 1885: 'As for my getting married, I have no bride as yet. If only I could find a really suitable, dear girl!' But all the winsome teenagers he approached found him unattractive and rarely took his offers of marriage with any seriousness.

His life-long and deepest love, that for his 'dear God', affords the most important insight into his personality. His was no Pauline conversion, but an inborn, steadfast and undying faith. He lived in two worlds, the everyday one and the world of his meditations, in which, as Hans-Hubert Schönzeler has written,[1] 'he may have attained visionary realms which found their expression in his music'. For him God and the world of transcendent spirit were realities which he never questioned. From the quiet, firm state of grace which he was able to reach came both calm in his distress and renewed strength for creative work. It is recorded that he always prayed deeply before improvising and that in lessons his pupils would become aware that his attention was no longer with them. The Angelus was ringing, and he was praying. A mystic in an unmystical age, the thoughts of the spirit that filled him were the life-spring of his art.

[1] *Bruckner* (Calder and Boyars, 1970).

8 Critics and interpreters

The nineteenth century saw the childhood and adolescence of musical criticism. By the time of Bruckner's creative maturity it had all the worst characteristics of an early manhood: rashness, intolerance and ambition for power. In Vienna this was especially evident because the musical world was firmly divided between the partisans of Brahms and Wagner respectively. The effect of critical hostility on Bruckner's composing activities was not particularly marked. It was almost always the opinions and advice of his friends that led to his periods of creative distress, revising and dearth of original composition. But his personal life was tormented by the critics who railed at him; it made him nervous about performing or publishing his music in the way he had written it, and many of his letters reveal the misery and anguish he suffered at the hands of Hanslick and his adherents, who saw him as a bungling Simple Simon, writing Wagnerian works of chronic prolixity.

Even allowing for the extreme lengths to which a reviewer might go in those years of gleeful mud-slinging, it is difficult to be charitable towards Hanslick, who was in a position of such giddy power that he could make a statement like: 'When I wish to annihilate, then I do annihilate.' Tovey, a friend of Joachim and an enthusiastic advocate of Brahms, summed up Bruckner's grimmest enemy admirably: [1]

Hanslick . . . saw in Bruckner fair game. Wagner gave Hanslick only

[1] *Essays in Musical Analysis*, Vol. II (Oxford University Press, 1935).

too lenient a treatment when he immortalised him in Beckmesser, named Hans Lich in the first sketch of the poem of *Meistersinger*. Beckmesser at all events knew the rules he so humbly adored. I have read Hanslick's collected works patiently without discovering either in his patronage of Brahms or in his attacks on Wagner, Verdi, Bruckner, the early works of Beethoven, Palestrina's *Stabat Mater*, or any other work a little off the average Viennese concert-goer's track in 1880, any knowledge of anything whatever. The general and musical culture shown in Hanslick's writings represents one of the unlovelier forms of parasitism; that which, having the wealth to collect *objets d'art* and the birth and education to talk amusingly, does not itself attempt a stroke of artistic work, does not dream of revising a first impression, experiences the fine arts entirely as the pleasures of a gentleman, and then pronounces judgment as if the expression of its opinion were a benefit and a duty to society.

Hanslick's criticism is not just damning, it is glossed over with smooth sarcasm and fatuous insincerity:

We have no wish to hurt this composer for whom we entertain a high regard both as man and artist and whose musical aims are sincere, albeit their treatment is strange.

Like every one of Bruckner's works, the E major symphony contains ingenious inspirations, interesting and even pleasant details—here six, there eight bars—but in between the lightnings there are interminable stretches of darkness, leaden boredom and feverish over-excitement.

When J. A. Vergeiner of Freistadt informed Bruckner that he intended to write an article about him in a paper, the composer wrote: 'Please do not write anything against Hanslick for my sake. His fury is dreadful. He is in a position to annihilate other people. With him one cannot fight. One can only approach him with petitions, but even that is of no use to me, because to me he is never at home.' At the end of a letter to Nikisch of 23rd November 1888, he wrote, 'Hanslick!!! Bülow!!! Joachim!!! For God's sake! I work as much as possible!'

Bruckner's protagonists were able to get their own back from time to time, and in no less forceful language. Hugo Wolf declared that 'one single cymbal crash by Bruckner is worth all the four symphonies of Brahms with the serenades thrown in'. A number of musical journals and the critics Speidel and Helm championed Bruckner, especially in the last fifteen years of his life. But, to turn aside from polemics, it is not hard to appreciate that vast sections of the musical public, reared on the Viennese classics and Mendelssohn, Schumann and Brahms, could not grasp the huge symphonic statements that Bruckner patiently unfolded. These works shattered previously held conceptions and therefore made slow progress, especially outside German-speaking countries.

Two men who had ruffled Bruckner's creative calm later became converts. Bülow, who wrote many sarcastic references to him in his letters and declared in 1888 that his symphonies were 'the anti-musical ravings of a half-wit', relented in 1891 when he called the *Te Deum* a splendid work, worthy of public performance. In 1877 Bruckner called Hans Richter 'the generalissimo of deceit'. Richter tried to have the best of both worlds in Vienna and was at that time giving the first performances of the Brahms symphonies. He was on occasions insincere to Bruckner but in later years, when the tide had turned in Bruckner's favour and Brahms's symphonic output was exhausted, he gave a great many performances of his works. Other notable conductors of Bruckner's works during his lifetime included Levi, Felix Mottl, Nikisch, Löwe and Anton Seidl, and in the first half of this century, Bruno Walter, Hans Knappertsbusch, Wilhelm Furtwängler, Jascha Horenstein and Otto Klemperer.[1]

Mahler's piano-duet arrangement of the Third Symphony delighted Bruckner, who presented him with the manuscript score of the work. Mahler was a keen if discriminating admirer

[1] See note to Bibliography for some recordings of notable Bruckner interpreters.

of Bruckner and the two men corresponded while Mahler was in Hamburg. After Bruckner's death Mahler continued to champion him, performing the Symphonies 4, 5 and 6 in Vienna, 1899–1901, and all the symphonies in New York, 1908. Although his attitude towards Bruckner, and also to Hugo Wolf and Richard Strauss, became more critical in his later years, he made an arrangement with Universal Edition in 1910 that all royalties on his works should go towards publication of and propaganda for Bruckner's music.

Bruckner criticism in the early years of this century took some time to shake off 'the ghost of old Klingsor', Wagner, whose influence on Bruckner's style was exaggerated in books such as that of Rudolf Louis (Munich, 1905). Max Auer wrote a book in angry response to this but it did not appear in print until 1923. August Göllerich, the official biographer, who was responsible for many performances of Bruckner's music, including the lesser-known works, died in 1922 having completed only a few chapters. Auer then saw the long four-volume study through the press and it was completed in 1936. Meanwhile the books of Orel, Kurth and Halm lifted the Wagnerian veil, and the popularization of Bruckner (hampered by the lack of 'saleable' works like songs or piano pieces) was under way on an international scale.

9 The problem of the revisions

In determining which versions of Bruckner's works represent the composer's true intentions a complicated and confusing series of problems arises, not equalled in the case of any other composer. The purpose of this chapter is to unfold as clearly and simply as is possible the history of the various revisions, versions and editions, without exploring the ramifications of each individual text—a task that would be beyond the scope of this book.[1]

Bruckner was a perfectionist when it came to his scores, which are clear and precise in layout. It was natural for him to revise a work more than once after completing it and he did so habitually from his first to his last creative years. It is not revisions such as these that present the problem. Johann Herbeck, after mighty efforts, succeeded in persuading him to make considerable alterations to the Third Symphony for its 1876 performance. Joseph Schalk and Ferdinand Löwe then persuaded him to agree to changes in orchestration and other details in the Seventh Symphony in 1883. But the most disastrous period of revision occurred after Levi's rejection of the Eighth Symphony in 1887. Joseph Schalk aided him in the revision of this work, and Franz Schalk assisted in the recomposition of the Third. It should be clearly stated that the Schalk brothers, Löwe, and others who aided Bruckner did so out of a genuine wish to further the

[1] For further details Deryck Cooke's series of articles, 'The Bruckner Problem Simplified' (*Musical Times*, Jan., Feb., April, May and Aug. 1969), should be consulted. I agree with his conclusions.

composer's recognition and his chances of performance and publication. To this end they worked devotedly for many years. The tragedy lies in the fact that these friends were pronounced Wagnerians, and while they loved Bruckner's music, they seriously misunderstood his language and mode of expression. However, Bruckner's rather malleable attitude to his friends' suggestions was seen by them as the indication of a free hand to bring out their own editions in print. In the process of this they transformed Brucknerian economy of scoring into Wagnerian luxury. They cut out portions, and freely altered tempo and expression marks, barring, dynamics and phrasing. Indeed the worst excesses, such as Franz Schalk's edition of the Fifth Symphony and Löwe's edition of the Ninth, involved the actual recomposition of extended passages.

Bruckner naturally protested about much of this but no one listened to him. To no avail he wrote letters begging that whatever might happen in performance, his published scores should not be altered, and he refused to give the approval of his signature to the Schalk-Löwe version of the Fourth Symphony. By 1903, as Deryck Cooke has shown,[1] there were twenty-five different scores of Bruckner's nine symphonies in existence, including his own original versions and revisions, and the scores of his friends. Of the ten published scores that this figure includes not one represented the composer's real thoughts.

Over thirty years after Bruckner's death the International Bruckner Society, under the presidency of Max Auer, began the project of publishing his works in their original form. This idea met not only with scepticism but with hostility, and with the strong opposition of Franz Schalk. In 1932, however, a year after Schalk's death, a performance of both versions of the Ninth Symphony in the same concert overcame almost all doubts, and a complete edition was begun under the editorship of Robert Haas, assisted by Alfred Orel. The Nazi Government then saw

[1] ibid.

the opportunity to use the International Bruckner Society as an unwitting tool for their propaganda. This seriously harmed the Society's reputation, and in 1945 Robert Haas was replaced as editor by Leopold Nowak. Up to that time Haas had issued all the symphonies (with the exception of the Third), the Missa Solennis, the Requiem, the E minor Mass and the D minor Mass. Now Nowak brought out an entirely new set of all the symphonies and major choral works, and in many cases his editorial view conflicted with that of Haas.

The devoted work of Haas and Nowak has brought the symphonies of Bruckner to the public in a form closer to his intentions than would have seemed possible in the early years of this century. Both editors have sarried out their tasks with irreproachable integrity. But the question remains, Haas or Nowak? It is my view that the editions of Haas are on the whole more Brucknerian in spirit. He has admirably fulfilled his intention of providing performing versions of high artistic worth. Nowak's attitude is undoubtedly the more scientific, and has resulted in an edition distinguished by the quality of its musicology. In the following chapters of this book, the editions of Haas will be referred to in order to avoid continual cross-references.[1] Therefore a word or two must be said here about the most important divergencies in Nowak's editions.

In the cases of Symphonies No. 1, No. 5, No. 6 and No. 9, the E minor Mass and the Requiem, Nowak's editions are virtually identical to those of Haas, and are mainly concerned with correcting small errors and oversights. With the Fourth Symphony and the F minor Mass he incorporates new material which has recently come to light. His edition of the Second Symphony (1877 version) undoubtedly contains influences of Herbeck, while Haas tried to get back to Bruckner's individual intentions. Nowak states that Haas confused the 1873 and 1877

[1] In the case of the Third Symphony, which Haas did not edit, the edition of Fritz Oeser (Brucknerverlag, 1950) is recommended.

versions. 'Haas' here has the more authentic ring, while 'Nowak' retains much that is unsatisfactory.

The Third Symphony is the most complex of all, and there is no satisfactory version of it. Oeser's edition of the 1878 version seems preferable to Nowak's reproduction of the Bruckner-Schalk score of 1889. The 1889 version contains a number of recomposed, re-orchestrated passages, the effect of which is to graft the more complex style of his later years on to the simpler style of the early 1870s. It is severely cut, and again the influence of friends is strongly evident.

In the Seventh Symphony Nowak includes orchestral alterations that Bruckner made for the first performance by Nikisch. These do not matter very much, but it seems unfortunate that Nikisch's 'conductor's markings' (approved by Bruckner for the same performance) were also retained, as they can interrupt the flow of the music unless the conductor takes great care. Haas incorporated elements of the 1887 version of the Eighth Symphony in his edition of the 1890 score, in a conjectural attempt to remove the influence of Joseph Schalk. The result is eminently Brucknerian and a very satisfying piece of creative editing. Nowak, true to his scientific approach, has issued the 1887 and 1890 versions separately. His edition also includes Symphony No. 0, the String Quartet, String Quintet and Intermezzo, Mass in D minor, *Te Deum* and Psalm 150.

10 Conception of Mass and symphony

Bruckner was born in a Romantic age and, it has often and quite rightly been remarked, that is almost all he had in common with it. Both his outward personality and his musical style are out of keeping with the typical image of the nineteenth-century composer. He seems rather to embody the habits and manner, if not exactly the style, of a Baroque or even late Renaissance master. His immense contrapuntal skill, his virtuosity at the organ, his ability to incorporate archaic forms in his own forward-looking idiom and his devotion to Sechter's theories are all reflections of this. He was attracted to music of the Baroque era, and his love for it is echoed in the primitive lustre of his brass writing, the boldness and width of his designs, and the naïve joy in polyphony that is magnificently conveyed in all the larger mature sacred works and which finds its symphonic culmination in the finale of Symphony No. 5. The rich splendour of his symphonic brass writing is clearly a development of his early predilection for brass instrumentation. Something of the magnificence of antiphonal brass writing associated with St Mark's Cathedral in Venice in the Renaissance era lives on in Bruckner's early music, for example in the unfinished Mass of 1846, the Requiem (1849), the Cantata *Auf Brüder, auf, zu frohen Feier* (1852—with six-part brass), Psalm 114 (1853—with three trombones), *Vor Arneths Grab* (1854—with three trombones) and the 'Libera' in F minor (1854, also with trombones). There is also a short, chorale-like and richly harmonized movement for trombones alone, *Aequale*, of 1847.

The three great Mass settings in D minor, E minor and F minor of the 1860s encompass the first period of Bruckner's creative maturity. Those in D minor and F minor are symphonic Masses in the tradition of Beethoven's *Missa Solennis* and Cherubini's Requiem Masses. The predominant influence upon them is the Viennese Classical Mass as perfected by Haydn and Mozart, but the Baroque element is never far from sight. The combined influence of Bach, the Viennese Classical composers and the dramatic Mass style of Beethoven gives Bruckner's Masses a depth of devotional character not paralleled in the sacred works of his contemporaries. There is no evidence that the sacred works of Liszt influenced Bruckner at this or any other time (although this has been suggested), but the two men shared an interest in plainsong which is strongly evident in each of Bruckner's Masses and pervades many sacred works of Liszt.

The essential feature of the Masses in D minor and F minor is the symphonic element, which in both works fuses the various contrasting sections of the Mass into one unified whole. This is not achieved at the expense of harmonic and melodic enhancement of individual sections of the text. Instead the symphonic conception creates unity in diversity. The orchestra plays an important role in the overall texture and often has themes of its own which are developed in truly symphonic style. One of the predominant features of Bruckner's symphonies is the thematic linking of the outer movements, and frequently the main theme of the opening movement returns in a triumphant statement in the last bars of the finale. This has its roots in these Masses, where there are reminiscences of the Kyrie in the 'Dona nobis pacem'—a traditional feature of Mass composition. In the Agnus Dei of the Mass in D minor the first Kyrie theme appears both at the opening and at the close, scale motifs which pervade much of the Mass are strongly evident, and the 'miserere' theme from the Gloria, the 'Amen' fugue subject of the Gloria, and the 'Et vitam venturi' theme from the Credo are quoted. In this procedure lie the seeds of the quotations in the finales of Symphonies 3, 4, 5 and 8. The use of fugue to heighten tension towards the end of Symphony No. 5 and the String Quintet may also stem from the final sections of the Glorias of all three Masses and the Credo of the F minor Mass.

Specific fingerprints of Bruckner's later symphonic style can also be pointed out in the Masses. The endings of the Gloria and Credo in both the D minor and F minor Masses have a definite feeling of the close of a symphonic movement. The Hosanna of the Benedictus of the D minor Mass has an exuberant yet characteristically abrupt close followed by a rest. This effect is used several times in the Masses and is designed to exploit fully a fine cathedral acoustic. Similar moments in the symphonies (such as the pauses after the mighty brass chords near the opening of Symphony No. 5) show that Bruckner had the same resonant acoustic effect in mind. Many harmonic and melodic features of the Masses, such as step-wise, parallel movements of parts in a climax, pedal points, a fondness for leaps of the sixth and octave and broad statements of the full tonic major, are personal characteristics of the composer that abound in his symphonies. The most obvious link between Mass and symphony is found in the many quotations from these three great Masses in the Symphonies 0, 2, 3 and 9. These and other 'cross-quotations' are another feature of Bruckner's style which will be discussed in their proper place.

When Bruckner turned from symphonic Mass to monumental symphony he was making no concession to popular mid-nineteenth-century taste. Both had long been declining in fashion. Wagner had declared that the symphonic conception of Beethoven's Ninth and the great Schubert C major was extinct. The symphonies of Berlioz and Liszt were vast canvases of programme music, and those of Mendelssohn and Schumann were confined both within the symphonic limitations of those composers and within the bounds of the Romantic lyrical world they explored.

Brahms had so far written none, but by the time Bruckner made his first real impression on the musical world (i.e. in the mid-1880s) Brahms was fully successful and established. Bruckner's very originality dispenses with the necessity to comment further on his relationship to any of these men, with the exceptions of Schubert (with whom he had a number of stylistic affinities which will shortly be discussed) and Beethoven, who provides a starting point for Bruckner in one particular work, namely the Choral Symphony. However, Beethoven's Ninth was not a model that Bruckner copied in an automatic way. It was instead a dramatic discovery which filled out his stream of thought and after which he shaped his own path with renewed individuality. He learned from it, but never imitated it so slavishly as has sometimes been stated. It may have suggested to him a mould, but what filled the mould was as far removed from the original as late Beethoven was from early Haydn.

The most serious charge laid against Bruckner's symphonic conception is that it is 'formless'. This is a justified comment if levelled against the first published versions, which, with their many transformations and cuts, fully deserve such a verdict. But to label the original versions of these works 'formless' is clearly a proof of Dryden's wisdom: 'By education most have been misled: So they believe, because they were so bred.' The lazy musical analyst, eyes open only to the truths of sonata form, can cope with Beethoven and Brahms. Faced with the obstacle of Bruckner in his path, he can only excuse his shortsightedness and impatience by pronouncing the works 'formless'. Certainly Bruckner struggled with problems of form and did not entirely overcome them until he wrote Symphony No. 5 (his seventh symphonic work). This was not the result of a misunderstanding of Classical sonata form, but a slow yet Herculean unfolding of his own originality. He could not build his city in a day, nor could he have built it at all had his slow unfolding been the result of mere ineptitude in coping with basic construction. We do not dismiss *Othello* because of the demerits of *Titus Andronicus.*

With each Bruckner symphony there is an intensification of vision. Again the lazy analyst will conclude that they are all much the same, rather like plaster-cast models differentiated by only a few outward transformations—the work of an impoverished artist with a mania for repetition. Again this conclusion is the voice of a critic, obviously deaf but not, unfortunately, dumb, who cannot comprehend a creative development that does not follow the clear, step-wise logic of Beethoven's pattern. Bruckner had only one symphonic conception and this was developed organically, overcoming problems with each new work in a more complete and satisfactory way, and unfolding new ideas which would flower in his next symphony. Symphonies 1 and 2 are the first stage in this process of organic development. Symphony No. 3 uncovers the most important roots of Bruckner's style, and this and Symphony No. 4 gave him more work and involved more revision than any others. But they are not apprentice works, and their achievements belittle their weaknesses. They are products from a master's forge and he perfected his mould in Symphony No. 5, after which any kind of clear sub-division, as is possible in discussing Beethoven's creative periods, cannot be attempted.

Fingerprints of style and general comments on the overall shape of Bruckner's symphonic conception can be formulated, however. Of the four elements—rhythm, melody, harmony and orchestration—the last two are often cited as Wagnerian in derivation. Bruckner's orchestration is economical and frequently austere. The orchestra called for in Symphonies 1 and 2 is double woodwind, 4 horns, 2 trumpets, 3 trombones, 2 timpani and strings. Symphony No. 3 adds an extra trumpet, No. 4 adds one tuba, and No. 5 calls for 3 timpani. Only Symphonies 7, 8 and 9 involve triple woodwind (but without piccolo), 8 horns and 4 Wagner tubas. The Adagio of Symphony No. 8 includes harps (3 if possible) and 'exotic' percussion effects are confined to two cymbal and triangle crashes (there is also one at exactly the same point in Symphony No. 7 which is of questionable authenticity). The orchestral sound is never Wagnerian and there is the conspicuous absence in the modest forces listed above of Wagner's beloved bass clarinet and cor anglais. Wagner's orchestration is smoothly resonant and rich in instrumental colour effects. Bruckner, even when employing his fullest brass ensemble, is economical in his use of massed effects, and his orchestral technique relies more on a clear linear style than on the building-up of colour. His orchestration is built up in terraces reminiscent of an organist moving from one manual to another and adding new voices to highlight a line in his tapestry. It is hard and ascetic and clearly emphasizes the thematic sectionalization of the music in a way quite alien to the rich homogeneity and frequent lavishness of Wagner. Nor did Bruckner imitate *Tristan*. His harmony is as bold as Wagner's, even at points in the Mass in D minor (of pre-*Tristan* date), but is never reminiscent of him; and that he could be bolder than Wagner is well illustrated in Symphony No. 9, especially in the opening theme of the Adagio:

Wagner was clearly not Bruckner's model either in orchestration or in harmony. But he certainly learned from Wagner a number of techniques which found expression within the framework of his individual language. Among these are the profoundly emotional *espressivo* qualities of the string writing in his Adagios, the strong, arresting effect of pronounced brass entries and the concept of building up long harmonic paragraphs. These are general features common to the works of both men and yet they find expression in very different voices and contexts. To point to an overtly Wagnerian bar in a Bruckner symphony is thus a difficult task: perhaps only the odd *appoggiatura* or turn of phrase is left to suggest Bayreuth. The opening themes of Bruckner's symphonies from No. 3 onwards do have a *Leitmotiv* quality, but it requires a tortuous stretching of definitions to equate their subsequent development with Wagnerian technique.

Bruckner uses a characteristic rhythm, ♩ ♩ [3: ♩ ♩ ♩] or [3: ♩ ♩ ♩] ♩ ♩, with such frequency from Symphony No. 2 (where it appears in dotted rhythm) onwards, that it has become known as 'the Bruckner rhythm'. This rhythmic pattern could well have its orgin in the frequent two-four and three-four bar sequences of the Upper Austrian folk music he knew so well.

Syncopation is another rhythmic device that adds variety to a number of passages and enhances their forward motion, for example the 'Et incarnatus est' and 'Crucifixus' sections of the Mass in F minor, the Adagio of Symphony No. 3 (before letter C) and the first movement of Symphony No. 5 (letter F). Even more characteristic is Bruckner's fondness for starting a theme with a rest at the beginning of the bar, for example the opening theme of the Adagio of Symphony No. 6, the 'second theme' of the first movement of No. 4, and the 'second themes' of the Adagios of Nos. 7 and 9, and in many other instances.

Bruckner's phrase-lengths are predominantly of four and eight bars. In his weaker moments these can become unrelentingly tedious (a weakness not unique among Teutonic composers), but this is in most cases avoided by the richness and variety of detail that his phrase-groups contain. The harmonic content and the 'rhythm' in which the harmony moves help to redeem the regularity of the phrase-lengths. Four-bar phrases are part of Bruckner's language and they are tiny units in the massive span of his slowly unfolding movements. There is a far greater variety of phrase-lengths in Symphonies 1 and 2—that is, before his vast symphonic conception took its first great step forward with Symphony No. 3.

Another general characteristic of Bruckner's style is his process of building a climax by means of sequential repetition. A Bruckner climax is a very individual thing, repeated phrases towering inexorably with almost cataclysmic effect. The real summit of each movement is enhanced by the way in which several previous pinnacles are averted and a new build-up started each time. Thus the ultimate culmination of these repeated periods of tension and release is remarkably effective. Bruckner's familiar unison themes always have a climactic character—for example the first movements of Symphony No. 9 (letter C) and Symphony No. 6 (after letter F).

His use of counterpoint in his symphonies is unobtrusive and unacademic. A great number of his themes invert, and many themes appear together with their own inversions. Often themes are developed in augmentation with their inversions in original note-values as a counterpoint. Diminution and *fugato* are also frequent procedures, contrapuntal lines being subtly dovetailed. Many of Bruckner's themes are 'double themes' and many of these are interlaced with new contrapuntal intricacies as they develop. A letter to Franz Bayer of 22nd April 1893 confirms that he felt symphonic counterpoint should be unobtrusive: 'I'm no pedal-point pusher—I don't give much for all that.

Counterpoint isn't genius, only a means to an end. And it's given me plenty of trouble.' His melodic style reveals a fondness for dotted rhythms, scale progressions, and leaps, often of the fifth, sixth and octave. One of his most striking melodic types is the chorale, and chorale passages in the symphonies always have an important role to play. He was familiar with Lutheran chorales through his study of Bach, the works of other Baroque composers and Sechter. He may also have been influenced by Mendelssohn's use of the chorale in his *Lobgesang*, *St Paul* and 'Reformation' Symphony. But he never used existing chorale melodies, only chorale-like themes of his own invention. They appear either in the majesty of full brass or as a sublimely restful idea in the 'second group' of themes, and they occur in most of the symphonies after No. 3. Thematic unity has already been mentioned and will be illustrated in the discussion of the various symphonies. The culmination of themes in the finale is not the only example of this, however, and in the major-key symphonies (4, 5, 6 and 7) especially there are several examples of quotations of themes in other movements.

Pauses have become almost a notorious element in Bruckner's symphonies. At the first performance of Symphony No. 2 a member of the Vienna Philharmonic Orchestra dubbed it the *Pausensinfonie*. Here again the pauses are an integral part of Bruckner's individual style. He replied to criticism of them by saying: 'Whenever I have something new and important to say, I must stop and take a breath first.' Naturally these pauses interrupt the flow of the music, but they are calculated to create a sense of anticipation and tension. They do not indicate a lack of ability to make a good transition, for excellent transitions can be found by only a cursory glance at the later Adagios; they emphasize the formal structure and can have either a dramatic or a wistful effect.

It is not possible to codify the form of Bruckner's symphonic movements. Any attempt to do so would have to qualify every statement made, as no symphony follows quite the same pattern as any other. Certain characteristics can be outlined, however. All the symphonies open quietly; Nos. 2, 4, 7, 8 and 9 with a *tremolando* and Nos. 3 and 6 with an *ostinato*. No. 5 has a slow introduction but the Allegro begins with a *tremolando*. Most of the first themes that emerge from this background of mystery are statements of fundamental harmonies, and the wonder lies in the fact that this 'formula' has a totally different character in each symphony. Nor do any of them sound like the prelude to *Das Rheingold*, although they share with it the evocation of creation itself, for example the opening of Symphony No. 4:

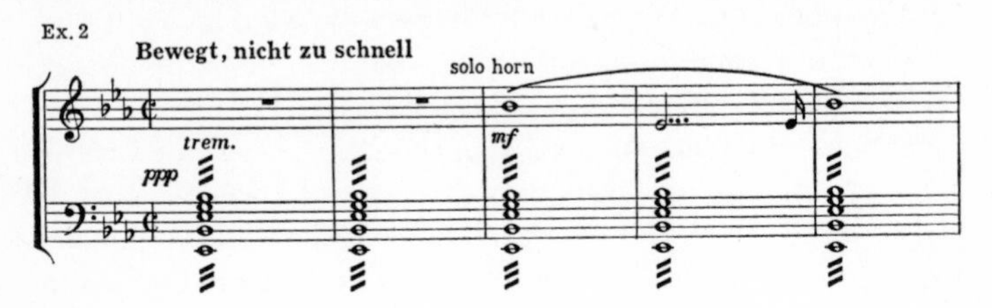

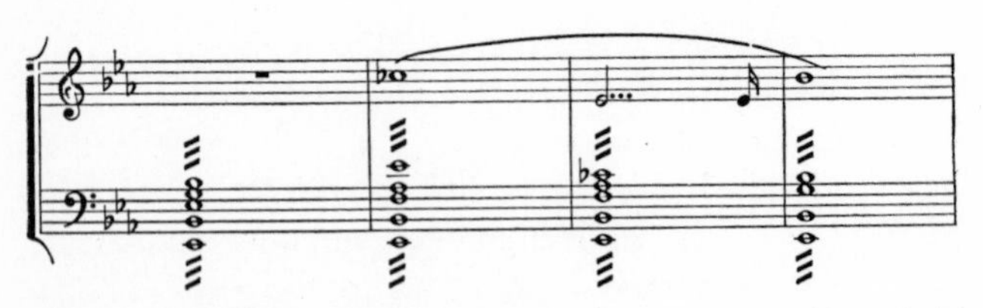

The finales of Nos. 6 and 7 begin with a *tremolando* and those of Nos. 2, 3, 4 and 8 with an *ostinato*.

Care and discretion must be taken in applying the terminology of sonata form to Bruckner's movements. We can for convenience refer to a 'first group' and 'second group' of themes, so long as we do not expect Bruckner to follow the classical pattern even in his expositions. A third thematic group becomes steadily more important and like the other two groups is composed of strongly contrasted material, although in some cases it is thematically related to them. In the finale of Symphony No. 2 the pattern of transition from exposition to development, which Bruckner follows in every succeeding outer movement, emerges. After a gigantic cadence marking the end of the first main section of the movement, the music remains still for a moment, ruminating gently on the foregoing thematic material, and so the development begins with slowly unfolding energy. A further word must be added about the second and third groups of themes. Bruckner's own term for his lyrical second group was *Gesangsperiode,* and themes in this group sometimes appear simultaneously, for example in the first movement of Symphony No. 3:

The third group sometimes takes the form of a unison or 'double unison' theme, for example in the first movement of Symphony No. 7:

In using the terms 'recapitulation' and 'coda' we must be even more cautious. The recapitulation is never an orthodox repeat, but a new version of the exposition raised to a higher plane. The coda is vastly extended and sums up everything in a mighty peroration. The second version of the first movement of Symphony No. 8 is the only outer movement to end quietly. From Symphony No. 3 onwards a process of telescoping the development and recapitulation begins, and finds its perfection in the first movement of Symphony No. 9, which defies any description of sonata form and can be discussed only in terms of Robert Simpson's apt phrase, 'statement, expanded counterstatement and coda'.

The Adagio movements do not have so many characteristics in common. In Symphonies 2 and 4 the slow movement is marked Andante, and in each symphony except Nos. 8 and 9 the slow movement follows the first movement. Most of the slow movements have two main thematic groups, and No. 6 is the only one in regular Brucknerian sonata form. The typical *Gesangsperiode* of the Adagios is a flowing lyrical idea which is embellished with ever richer accompaniment in its subsequent appearances.

The scherzos display the Austrian side of Bruckner most vividly. The earlier ones have the quality of peasant dances and the trio is frequently a *Ländler*. Here is an affinity with both Schubert and Mahler. The Austrian elements in Bruckner's music have been both praised and denigrated very much according to the personal taste of the critic. In the main his treatment of them is neither obvious nor predictable, and their scale is never so extended as to upset the balance of the whole symphony. The second theme of the Scherzo of Symphony No. 5 is a good example. It never has a run of more than twenty bars or so and never upsets the symphonic context of the movement in a way that might well have happened if Mahler had developed it. Bruckner's early experiences as a dance-band fiddler may find their artistic fulfilment in these early scherzos, but the symphonic aspects of these movements become more pronounced after Symphony No. 4. In the Scherzo of Symphony No. 9 no trace is left of a peasant dance: a new and very different world is explored.

Bruckner's scherzos are never programme music, but they represent the nearest point he approached to it. That of Symphony No. 4 is marked 'Hunting Scherzo'. He did provide 'programmes' for Symphonies 4 and 8, but these are in quite a different category and amount to feeble afterthoughts, written to please his Wagnerian friends (who could not conceive of non-programmatic music) and brim with romantic effusions such as dawn, shady forests, horsemen galloping forth, and so on. He revealed his genuine view on this subject after Joseph Schalk provided a pictorial explanation of Symphony No. 7 for a Vienna performance. Bruckner angrily exclaimed: 'If he has to write poetry, why should he pick on my symphony?'

Bruckner's treatment of tonality is best seen in the context of each individual work, but one or two general points may be made here. He had a fondness for Neapolitan relationships, finely illustrated in the String Quintet and Symphony No. 6, but evident in almost every mature work. Rapid changes of tonality are a feature of his sequences, which often rise in steps of a semitone. Harmony and tonality are his most striking points in common with Schubert. In both composers the key relationships between the first- and second-subject groups are unconventional. Mediant instead of dominant relationships are favoured and they both exploit sudden changes from major chords or tonalities to minor ones. For both men harmony was as much an agent of expression as melody and rhythm, and Bruckner's expansiveness of form is due to the enlarged modulatory possibilities of his style. 'Heavenly length', recurrence of themes, statements of the second group in two melodic strands and the Austrian quality of some melodies are further points in common with Schubert. They have very few resemblances in the realms of orchestration, counterpoint or rhythm. It is doubtful whether all the elements of kinship between Schubert and Bruckner were the direct result of Bruckner's knowledge of Schubert's work. In Bruckner's formative years Schubert's Masses and symphonies were unpopular, and his knowledge of Schubert was at that time largely confined to songs and piano music. But the strong affinity between these two composers lies at a deep level and cannot be explained in terms of direct influence.

Finally the difference between the symphonic conception of Bruckner and Mahler respectively ought to be considered. The two men were very different in personality and this is reflected in their scores. Mahler's life and character are dominated by *Weltschmerz*, pessimism, unrest, irony and a longing for escape. The programmatic element in Mahler's symphonies is important. Mahler was a complex, obsessive and searching religious mystic. Bruckner, his senior by thirty-six years, shares very little of all this. His faith was a mysticism of quite a different order. He had found his God, and with Him repose and serenity. However, Mahler undoubtedly inherited a number of superficial points of style from Bruckner. These include the rustic elements found in the earlier scherzos of both composers, long song-like melodies as in Bruckner's 'second-group' themes, a fondness for rugged, stubborn march rhythms and the symphonic time-scale. But in the realms of expression, orchestration and general symphonic shape there is a vast gulf between Bruckner and Mahler. An Austrian symphonist nearer to Bruckner in style is Franz Schmidt (1874–1939). Schmidt's four symphonies should be far better known and in some respects they are worthy successors to Bruckner's nine. He studied at the Vienna Conservatorium, 1889–96, and was a pupil of Bruckner, but for only a very short time.

11 Smaller works—chamber music

Bruckner composed over thirty male-voice choruses in addition to a number of secular works for mixed chorus. They are of little concern to the non-German listener and do not represent important stages in Bruckner's creative unfolding. They are the side-products of his art; pieces that could be readily and frequently performed. Most of them were written for specific choral groups. The most important male-voice choruses include *Am Grabe* (1861), *Germanenzug* (1863), *Das deutsche Lied* (1892) and a symphonic chorus with orchestra, *Helgoland* (1893). *Helgoland* was the only secular vocal composition that Bruckner included in his bequest to the Hofbibliothek. *Am Grabe* was the first work written for the *Liedertafel 'Frohsinn'* after his appointment as conductor. It has the distinction of being his first work to be performed in Linz and to receive a press notice in the *Linzer Zeitung*: 'The entire composition is imbued with tender emotion and unshakeable faith in God.' Perhaps *Abendzauber* (1878) is the best example of the whole genre to mention, as it sums up the purely Romantic spirit that they all share. It is set for baritone solo and three yodellers and the accompaniment consists of four horns. Austrian folk-elements abound in choruses such as this, and thus a tenuous link is formed with some of the symphonic scherzos.

The only direct link between Bruckner's many love-affairs and his creative work is found in the small group of songs and piano pieces that they inspired. The influence of Schubert and also of Schumann (whose songs he came to know at the time of his studies with Sechter) can be seen in the three songs of the late 1860s—*Im April, Mein Herz und deine Stimme* and *Herbstkummer*. The last, with its varied accompaniment, is the best of the group. The piano pieces are quite pleasant, very Austrian and undistinguished. They are mostly dance-like pieces except for the Fantasie in G (1868) with its slow introduction reminiscent of Liszt and oddly contrasting Allegro in rococo style, and *Erinnerung* of about the same date, which is an ambitious piece with interesting harmonies.

Bruckner is one of a relatively small number of great composers whose chief performing talent lay in the organ-loft. Unlike Franck or Reger, however, he has not left a single composition of any value for his instrument. The C minor Prelude and Fugue of 1847 has nothing more than Mendelssohn in it, and his last organ work proper, the D minor Fugue of 1861, is academic and uninspired. Sadly, we have no record of his famous improvisations, but these were to bear fruit in other, more significant ways. The organ was an essential stepping-stone for Bruckner's creative imagination.

The Overture in G minor of 1863 is the only orchestral work of interest in his output aside from the symphonies. It is an enormous improvement on the three short pieces for orchestra that slightly preceded it. Cast in straightforward sonata form, it has a slow introduction notable for its strong descending octaves, reminiscent of Mozart's *Jupiter* Symphony, striking harmonic suspensions and chromaticism. There is a fine example of a typical Bruckner crescendo or 'blaze-up' using the first-subject material (at figure 14 in the Universal Edition score). The second subject should be noted. Beginning on the dominant ninth chord of B flat major, this is only a glimmer of the *Gesangperioden* to come, but a glimmer that has the glance of hidden gold.

The String Quartet in C minor of the previous year is a delightful work, worthy of occasional performance, which was discovered only after World War II. It is, however, merely an advanced exercise in composition, showing that Bruckner had a firm grasp of traditional forms, proficiency in string-writing and a thoughtful way of developing thematic material.

His single important chamber work is the String Quintet in F major which he composed between Symphonies 5 and 6. It is by no means a 'symphony for five strings' and it never stretches the quintet medium beyond its capabilities, save perhaps for the last seventeen bars of the finale, where he is thinking too much in orchestral terms. The Quintet is unlike any other late nineteenth-century chamber music; though Brahms's Op. 88 (written two and a half years later in 1882) shares the key of Bruckner's, and the idea of contrapuntal devices in the finale, the two works have little in common. Yet Bruckner's Quintet is a worthy companion not only of the chamber music of Brahms but of late Beethoven and Schubert also. The Adagio is one of his most profound movements and illustrates perfectly how well at home he was in a chamber-music medium. Throughout the Quintet fascinating Neapolitan relationships abound. This is evident from the very outset; so many Bruckner movements hint, in their very first bars, at the tonality to be explored. Note the A flat and D flat in the first bar:

The flat submediant key, D flat, makes itself strongly felt throughout the whole work. F sharp or G flat major (the Neapolitan flat supertonic of F) is likewise important, and this is the key of the second thematic group of the first movement (letter

E). The Scherzo is in D minor and its first section ends on the dominant, A. B flat major immediately takes over, and both G flat and D flat are encountered before the final cadence in D major. The Trio then starts on the Neapolitan flat supertonic of D, E flat major, and its central section is in G flat, which is again the key of the Adagio. The order of movements was originally Adagio then Scherzo, but Bruckner altered their places and thus created a better approach to the finale.

Although the Scherzo is beyond any doubt the right movement for this Quintet, one feels almost grateful to Hellmesberger for objecting to it, as this brought forth the exquisitely graceful Intermezzo. Once again this movement (in D minor) contains some fine ebb and flow with G flat major.

12 The early symphonies in minor keys

The *Studiensymphonie* (Study Symphony) in F minor was never performed in Bruckner's lifetime and the composer regarded it as nothing more than an exercise. The work does have an occasional hearing nowadays, although set beside the Overture in G minor it is impersonal, stiff in movement, thematically uninspired and conventionally orchestrated. The brass writing and the use of triple woodwind reveal that Bruckner had responded to Kitzler's emphasis on the importance of orchestral colour, and the large scale of the work is characteristic of Bruckner's hand. The coda of the finale is one of the finest moments, reminiscent of the opening of Symphony No. 0 in its figuration, and containing a chorale-like motif later used in the Mass in D minor.

When Otto Dessoff rehearsed Bruckner's early Symphony in D minor with the Vienna Philharmonic Orchestra, he turned to the composer and asked him to tell him where the first subject of the opening movement was. This reception of the work may lie behind Bruckner's decision not to include it amongst his numbered symphonies. Yet No. 0 is a most individual work, a great step forward from the Symphony in F minor, and the opening which puzzled Dessoff is the first truly Brucknerian symphonic *ostinato*. He used it again to open Symphony No. 3, where it forms a background to the principal theme. The reason why Symphony No. 0 reveals Bruckner's personality so clearly is that, while it was written during the winter of 1863–4, it was thoroughly revised in 1869—that is, three years after

Symphony No. 1, and after his coming to know Beethoven's Ninth. The first movement is the most remarkable and shows many traces of his experience of Beethoven's last symphony, for example in the descending fifths and fourths at the opening over a drone of an open fifth. Another link with the Choral Symphony is the chromatic *ostinato* at the opening of the coda—a device which Bruckner was to use again in the first movement of Symphony No. 3 and also in the finale of Symphony No. 6, where it reappears literally as in No. 0. Other features to be noticed in this first movement are the excellent second group, and the beginning of the development which grows naturally out of the cadence of the exposition—a feature that finds further expression in the next symphony, No. 2 in C minor. No. 0 also shares with No. 2 the procedure of quotation from the sacred choral works. The staccato quavers from the 'Gratias' of the Mass in F minor propel the development of the first movement. The Andante includes two statements of the 'Qui tollis peccata mundi' from the Mass in E minor. The finale quotes the Osanna of the early Requiem in D minor (at letter A) and the seven-part setting of the 'Ave Maria' appears at the transition from development to recapitulation. The symphony itself was drawn on for thematic material in later symphonies.

Bruckner called his official Symphony No. 1 in C minor 'das kecke Beserl'—an untranslatable phrase, 'the saucy little besom' being the nearest equivalent—and this portrays in a nutshell the jaunty, cheeky character of the opening idea and the bold impetuosity of the Scherzo. Both the outer movements are faster in tempo than is usual in Bruckner's symphonies, and the boisterous spirit and vigour of the finale particularly justify the composer's later astonishment at the dash and daring of the piece. But again, there are many pointers to the later works to be observed here, and they mark the finest moments in the score. The second group of the first movement begins most effectively in uncomplicated two-part writing, is embellished in a restatement and leads to a characteristic *tutti*. Out of this *tutti* (which announces the rhythmic pattern of the main theme of the finale in the brass) emerges a strong idea in a broader tempo in E flat major (letter C) which, with its accompanying demisemiquaver figure, provides powerful building material for the development, after which it does not reappear. The transition to the recapitulation is a fine stroke, the home dominant key emerging for the first time in the movement, and the movement ends with idiosyncratic finality. The Adagio is in A flat major, but its opening gives no hint of this. Here is an inkling of the technique used in the Adagio of Symphony No. 9. The ambiguous harmony first gropes darkly towards F minor, then lifts twice in mysterious directions before any clear sign of the tonic key emerges. Only in the last eighteen bars does A flat major claim its rightful place and the movement closes in tranquillity. The G minor of the Scherzo and the G major of the Trio are fresh tonal realms, and so the impetuous outburst of the Scherzo is doubly unsuspected after the calm of the Adagio's final A flat major. In the finale there is a good example of Bruckner's technique of slowly building up energy at the beginning of the development after some reflections on the cadence figure of the exposition. The work ends with a chorale-like blaze of glory on the horns. The First Symphony is unique amongst its companions discussed in this chapter, in having no thematic allusions to the sacred choral works.

It is necessary to comment briefly on the 1891 version of the work ('Vienna' version), although the 'Linz' version is almost always played today, and even Nowak, who prefers the later revisions on the whole, has issued this symphony in its 1866 form. Bruckner did revise it of his own volition despite the fact that Bülow and Rubinstein had admired the Linz version and Levi even urged him not to alter his original ideas. He bequeathed both versions of the score to the Hofbibliothek. The main differences in the later score are found in harmony, counterpoint, scoring, texture, altered bar-periods, extra tempo-markings and the rewriting of certain sections, including the end of the finale. The result of all this was effectively to destroy the charm and natural exuberance of his youthful style.

Symphony No. 2 is also in C minor. This fact has actually been cited as a proof of Bruckner's naïvety as a composer. 'After all, who would write his first two symphonies in the same key?' sneers the enemy. Here, as so often, the enemy's zeal outstrips his intelligence. Just over five busy years separate the two works—years that saw the creation of the Masses in E minor and F minor and the writing of the definitive version of Symphony No. 0 in D minor. Furthermore the two symphonies share little more than their key-signature. The impetuous qualities of No. 1 find few echoes in No. 2. The slow deliberate mastery of later years is not yet achieved but the essence of Bruckner's style is far more apparent. Over a *tremolando* tonic chord the opening theme feels its way into C minor, and towards the end of its 23-bar span the trumpet throws out the 'Bruckner rhythm' in dotted values, on the note C. The whole theme is then expanded in a varied counterstatement. The 'Bruckner rhythm' never takes on a melodic shape during the symphony. Its use is structural in the first movement and the finale. The second groups of themes in both outer movements enjoy a few adventures of tonality. In the first movement the second group appears at first, quite properly, in E flat major. In the development it explores both G and A flat major before arriving in D flat major, and in the recapitulation finds a happy resting place in C major. In the finale the second group enters in A major, although the way prepared for it pointed to A flat. However, it effortlessly finds its way into E flat in its own measured time. It too appears in C major in the recapitulation, but here the delight is an even fresher surprise: it follows a dominant seventh chord of D flat major. Both second groups are characteristically lyrical, flowing and gentle. The third thematic group of the first movement restores the drive and impetus of the music with a stark double unison:

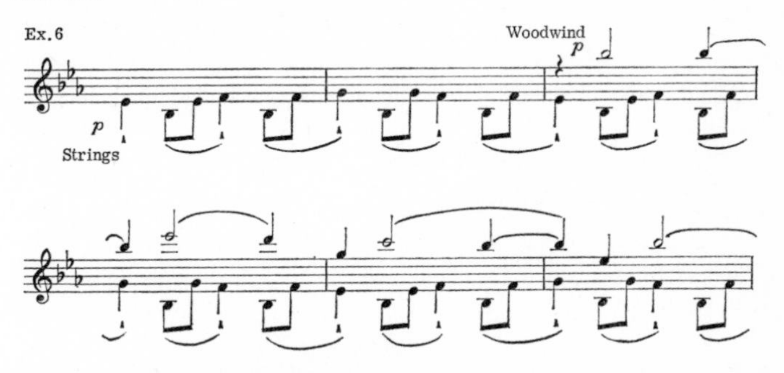

The *ostinato* figure from Ex. 6 takes on an augmented form in the development and appears over another *ostinato*. The coda, as in Beethoven's Ninth, begins over an *ostinato* bass.[1] Typically, the coda is two-fold. The first and greater part of it is development of the opening theme, and the second (at the final return of Tempo I) is a mighty *tutti* in C minor.

The Adagio clearly illustrates Bruckner's process of enhancing the restatements of themes by elaborating and enriching the accompanying figuration. There are two quotations from the Benedictus of the Mass in F minor. The finale has two similar quotations from the Kyrie of the same Mass and is linked to the first movement in a number of ways. The *ostinato* figure with which it opens is derived from the opening theme of the symphony; this theme itself appears during the development, first in a transformed version, then in its original form and finally grows into a new melody. It also finds its place in the coda. The 'Bruckner rhythm' also links the outer movements, appearing at a number of climactic points including the final C major

[1] The optional cut suggested here should never be observed as it would take us too quickly and uncertainly to C minor and upset the proportions of the movement. The same logic applies to the optional cuts towards the end of the finale.

peroration. The explanation of the pauses and of the less daring character of this symphony lies in Dessoff's criticism of Symphonies 0 and 1. The pauses were Bruckner's attempt at emphasizing his formal structure: they in no way detract from the greatness of the work. He has now climbed the foothills: the Himalayas lie ahead.

That new territory is to be explored is obvious from the beginning of Symphony No. 3 in D minor, where the broad tempo and extended thematic dimensions at once suggest a different time-scale. After four bars in which a multiple *ostinato* grows, the trumpet announces the principal subject:

The horn then expands this figure and a *crescendo* leads to an important unison idea, which is immediately restated in rich harmonies. One of the most captivating features of this first movement is the way in which this motif recurs, always in a new harmonization. Its first unison entry follows thirty bars of tonic pedal. This is a feature of Bruckner's openings that will be observed again. The restatement of the opening material is in the dominant key, again over a pedal bass, and the second group (see Ex. 3) is also characterized by a held pedal bass. This second group contains the 'Bruckner rhythm' (which was implied in the first theme) and, using this, a *crescendo* leads to the third theme, a firm unison which also shares the 'Bruckner rhythm'. Shortly before the development, there is a brief quotation of the 'Miserere' from the Mass in D minor, and in the transition to the development a theme from Symphony No. 2 appears. Towards the end of the exposition, and during the remainder of the movement, Ex. 7 is stated in inversion and augmentation, and in canon using both of these devices. The Adagio is spoiled by its uninteresting thematic material and relentless one-, two- and four-bar phrases, yet it has a noble climax—the worthy predecessor of those in almost all succeeding symphonies. At the end of the movement there is a reminiscence of the sleep motif from Act III of *Die Walküre*, and there is a whiff of smoke from Loge's magic fire in the finale (bar 301f). This is the 'Wagner Symphony', which contained a number of Wagner quotations in its first draft. The Scherzo is a finely knit movement and, along with the Trio, it will appeal to listeners with a predilection for the *Ländler*. In the Adagio some use is made of a cadence common in Viennese Classical sacred music:

Bruckner had previously used this *Marienkadenz* in the four-part 'Ave Maria' of 1856, the seven-part 'Ave Maria' of 1861, the Agnus Dei of the Mass in F minor and the piano piece *Erinnerung* of 1868.

The second theme of the finale appears surprisingly in F sharp major. It is a double theme; the strings play a polka while the horns intone a chorale. August Göllerich recalls an occasion when Bruckner commented on this unusual combination. He and Bruckner were walking past a house in the Schottenring one evening and they overheard dance music. Not far away the body of the cathedral architect Schmidt lay in the Sühnhaus. Bruckner remarked: 'Listen! In that house there is dancing, and over there the master lies in his coffin—that's life. It's what I wanted to show in my Third Symphony. The polka represents the fun and joy of the world and the chorale represents the sadness and pain.'

The principal weakness of the outer movements of this symphony is a problem of form. With this work the process of telescoping the development and recapitulation begins, and Bruckner's misjudgment here is that neither the opening movement nor the finale has a successful recapitulatory climax. In both movements the recapitulation is forestalled by a massive statement of Ex. 7 in the development section in the tonic key. In both cases the momentum of the rest of the movement is destroyed and all the ensuing climaxes have a weak effect. The 1890 version of the symphony (as edited by Nowak) fails to solve these structural weaknesses. Several of the *tutti* passages are altered in the later score with some success, but few of the 'improvements' are impressive. Rescoring of brass-parts, altering of bar-periods, large cuts and a bombastic coda to the finale amount to the loss of a number of fine effects and the gain of nothing but a desire to hear Ex. 7 draw the work to an end.

13 Sacred vocal works

Bruckner completed seven Masses including his Requiem. The first two of these date from the early 1840s and are typical examples of the short provincial Austrian *Landmesse* of the day. The Mass in C major, of about 1842, is for alto, two horns and organ, the organ accompaniment being written as a figured bass. Parts of the text are cut, particularly the Credo. Like every Mass which followed, this early example shows the use of themes influenced by plainsong, and chromaticism for pictorial effect. The opening of the Credo is a plainsong quotation, while only a few bars later, at the words 'qui propter nostram salutem descendit de coelis', Bruckner gives a chromatic response. The Benedictus contains a clear trace of Mozart's influence. The Mass in F major for Maundy Thursday of 1844 is very similar to the C major Mass and shows plainsong influence, but suffers even more from crippling local conditions. There is no Kyrie or Gloria but a Gradual, 'Christus factus est', and an Offertory, 'Dextera Domini fecit virtutem', are interpolated. A number of interesting points of imitation occur in the generally homophonic texture, and in the Osanna there are effective leaps of the seventh and a tendency towards dissonance and unorthodox modulation. The work is headed with the letters, so significant in later works, A.m.D.g.—Ad majorem Dei gloriam.

The fragment of an unfinished Mass in E flat major, for chorus, orchestra and organ, of about 1846, shows a more ambitious approach to choral and instrumental writing. There are antiphonal responses for soloists and chorus and the vocal parts are laid out in a less amateurish way. Of the motets of the 1840s, the two 'Asperges me' (1845) and the 'Tantum ergo' in A major deserve a mention. The first of the 'Asperges me' is an Aeolian setting that begins polyphonically; its companion, inspired by plainsong, is a hymn in two sections which flank a verse of unharmonized plainsong. The 'Tantum ergo' moves from A major to D sharp (enharmonic E flat major—the polar opposite of A) at the climax of a central imitative section and returns to A by way of B major.

With the Requiem in D minor, for soloists, chorus, orchestra and organ of 1848–9, we leave juvenilia behind. The key remained a significant one for Bruckner until his last symphony, and this Requiem may be regarded as his first truly notable composition, well worthy of performance. He always retained a regard for it and made some revisions to the score as late as 1894, commenting: 'It isn't bad.' Haydn and Mozart are his principal models, particularly Mozart's Requiem in the same key, to which there are a number of thematic allusions. The opening theme of the Requiem is almost identical to the opening of Mozart's. At 'donum fac remissionis' in Bruckner, Mozart's 'Ne absorbeat eas tartarus' is quoted, and at 'defunctorum de poenis' the theme of Mozart's 'de ore leonis' appears. But Bruckner's own voice is assuredly to the fore. Scored for three trombones, strings and organ continuo (with a horn replacing one trombone in the Benedictus), the orchestral effect is austere, yet the festal Mass style of his later mature period is anticipated. Dark string syncopations accompany the opening choral passage. 'Quam olim Abrahae' is a great double fugue using the unexpected key of F minor. The Benedictus and Agnus Dei particularly reveal profound depths of expression.

The Magnificat in B flat major of 1852 is also scored austerely for two trumpets, three trombones, strings and organ. It contains a fine fugal Amen. The settings of Psalms 22 and 114 also culminate in impressive fugues and both show the influence of Mendelssohn. Contrapuntal work distinguishes the 'Libera' in F minor of 1854, which makes dramatic use of trombones, low strings and organ. The next real landmark in the evolution of Bruckner's choral and orchestral style is the Missa Solennis in B flat minor. Here the influence of the Masses of Haydn and Mozart is still strong, and the composer's individuality is not so clearly evident as in the Requiem, although the Mass certainly deserves performance. Bruckner uses a richer orchestral palette in this work, which was partly an elaboration of sketches made in his Kronstorf years. The Credo contains a bold and dramatic use of chromaticism at 'Et resurrexit' and ends with a fine triple fugue at 'Et vitam venturi', which is thematically linked with the opening. This fugue has the characteristics of those in the three great Masses, such as inversion of the subject and an effective entry of the soloists just before the end.

As a farewell to St Florian Bruckner wrote an 'Ave Maria' in F major for soloists, mixed chorus and organ, dedicated to Ignaz Traumihler. This piece, which contains some fine chromatic moments, was the last sacred work before the period of study with Sechter, and all those that follow command more attention. Psalm 146 of 1860 uses a large orchestra and is in the style of a cantata. Two motets of 1861 illustrate that Bruckner had thoroughly mastered complex contrapuntal writing with Sechter. 'Afferentur regi' contains a characteristic leap in the bass part to a low A pedal note at 'et exsultatione'. The seven-part 'Ave Maria' is the first masterpiece among the motets—a fine piece of contrapuntal weaving clearly showing Bruckner's Palestrinian ancestry and yet allowing free reign to his own chromatic richness. The three-part female chorus enters alone, followed by the four-part male chorus, and then all parts join in a solemn climax (see Ex. 9 overleaf). Similar strength of harmonic device can be seen in Psalm 112 for double chorus and orchestra of 1863.

Bruckner's first work of symphonic grandeur is the Mass in

Ex. 9
S
A
T
B
mf
San - cta Ma - ri - a, san - cta Ma -
San - cta Ma - ri - a,
San - cta Ma -
ff
- ri - a, san - cta Ma - ri - a,
san - cta Ma - ri - a, ma - - -
- ri - - a, san - cta Ma - ri - a,
ma - ter De - - - - - - i,
- - - ter De - - - - - - i,
ma - ter De - - - - - - i,

D minor of 1864, a traditional Austrian festal Mass which he revised in 1876 and 1881. The opening of the Kyrie is a string passage over a tonic pedal, rich in dissonance and remote harmonies, but never straying away from D minor. The first Kyrie introduces an ascending scale that is a unifying element throughout the Mass, appearing at the opening of the Gloria and Sanctus, in descending form in the Benedictus, and in both forms in the Agnus Dei. The more imitative and varied second Kyrie contains an octave figure that is another link between the various movements and recurs in the Gloria, Credo and Sanctus. (Scale motifs and octave leaps are also a unifying feature of Psalm 150.) The first lines of both Gloria and Credo are reserved for plainsong intonation as in the Mass in E minor. The Gloria in D major opens dramatically with chromatic crotchet movement in the bass, soon replaced by pervading diatonic quaver scales. The central 'Agnus Dei' section of the Gloria opens in an unexpected A flat major, and the 'miserere' motif appears in both Symphonies 3 and 9. As in the E minor and F minor Masses, this movement ends with a fugue, which includes stretto and stretto by inversion. The symphonic elements are most clearly seen in the Credo, also in D major. The central 'et incarnatus est' section (Adagio) begins with a dramatic entry of the soloists in F sharp major. The vocal parts climb chromatically in a unison climax towards a D major six-three chord at 'ex Maria Virgine', and 'et homo factus est' cadences wonderfully in C major. After a vigorous 'Crucifixus', the entry of *pianissimo* organ and quiet solo voices at 'et sepultus est' is a most effective change of colour, and so is the dark descending chromatic figure at 'mortuorum' —an effect almost identical to the setting of that word in the Mass in F minor. 'Et resurrexit' is approached by way of a symphonic orchestral introduction of twenty-eight bars on the home dominant, almost reminiscent of Symphony No. 1 with its tramping bass *ostinato* and broken phrases of dotted quavers growing in momentum. The G major Benedictus has a sixteen-bar introduction of graceful poise, and flowing accompaniment and interludes enhance this pastoral movement. It hovers in C sharp major at the close, almost suggesting a vision of the Holy Spirit, when the chorus enter boldly with the reprise of the Hosanna in D. The thematic summing-up of all that has gone before, in the Agnus Dei, has been discussed in Chapter 10.

The Mass in E minor of 1866 is the most individual and perhaps the finest of the three great Masses of this period, and stands apart from almost all other nineteenth-century liturgical music by virtue of the forces it employs and its peculiarly expressive harmonic and contrapuntal language. The authentic performing version is that of 1882, which followed two revisions, of 1869 and 1876. The Mass employs an eight-part mixed chorus and a wind band of two oboes, two clarinets, four horns, two trumpets and three trombones—a notable combination making no use of timpani, organ or soloists and not paralleled in any other Bruckner work. This orchestra is used sparingly in a background role, yet it contributes wonderfully to the striking contrasts of texture and constant variety of sound. In the Gloria the opening bassoon arpeggio figure sets in motion the forward-moving repeated crotchet pattern that propels the whole structure, while step-wise and repeated quaver patterns perform a similar function in the Credo. In the Benedictus and Agnus Dei the orchestra weaves its own threads into the intricate texture of the tapestry and forms an unbroken link between the vocal phrases, while in the Kyrie and Christe and at the climax of the Sanctus it powerfully reinforces and highlights moments of the vocal declamation of the text.

No work of Bruckner's illustrates so succinctly his unique position amongst composers since the Baroque era. Here is music of profound wisdom conveyed with utmost simplicity of expression that embraces Romantic, fully Brucknerian harmony, bold motivic development and powerful choral and instrumental combinations, together with the devoutness, restraint, poignancy and austere power of the highest era of Italian Renaissance polyphony. It was keenly received by the Cecilian Movement, who saw in it a realization of their aim of reviving a Palestrinian *a cappella* style of church music to counter the secular and worldly tones that customarily accompanied mid-nineteenth-century sacred music. Bruckner's Mass is closest to the style of sixteenth-century vocal counterpoint in the Kyrie (which is in effect an *a cappella* movement, as the instrumental parts are optional) and the Sanctus. The latter is polyphony of consummate mastery, beginning with an eight-part canonic structure, based on a motif from Palestrina's *Missa brevis* (where it appears at the words 'rex facta'). At bar 27 the brass enter to crown the words 'Dominus Deus Sabaoth', which are powerfully and majestically announced on repeated *fff* chords. The cadence, to the words 'in excelsis', climbing to G major with the power of an apocalyptic vision, is coloured with the telling sonorous dissonances which enrich the harmony of the whole work from the third bar of the Kyrie onwards. Bruckner specially noted on his manuscript that both the Kyrie and Sanctus were to be conducted in four-four, thus ensuring their effect of unhurried dignity and awe.

No other Catholic church music of the Romantic era (with the exception perhaps of Liszt's late *Via Crucis*) combines intense expressiveness with such simplicity of means; the work foreshadows an almost twentieth-century concept of vocal and instrumental texture and intimate harmonic subtlety. The reserving of the words 'Gloria in excelsis Deo' and 'Credo in unum Deum' for plainsong intonation implies that Bruckner was thinking foremost of liturgical use for this Mass. Indeed the comparatively severe texture of the several *a cappella* sections gives it a firmer liturgical atmosphere than the Masses in D minor and F minor. However, the work would serve admirably in either liturgical or concert performance.

The mood and context of the text of each section of the Mass as always predestine Bruckner's musical response. Compare the firm homophonic movement of such a passage as 'Et resurrexit' from the Credo with the intense pleading of the contrapuntal 'miserere' from the Agnus Dei, with its anguished, widely leaping bass part. Sonata form is strictly followed in the Benedictus, yet the richness of the chromatic harmony is Bruckner's direct and characteristic emotional response to the words. The opening of the Kyrie is in the Phrygian mode, with chords hovering above a tonic pedal and expressively powerful *crescendi* leading to the more intense and contrapuntal 'Christe'. An example of a forthright use of counterpoint is found in the last section of the Gloria, a double fugue:

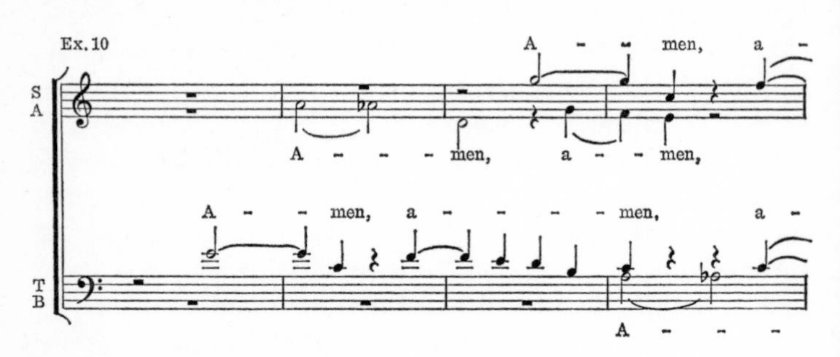

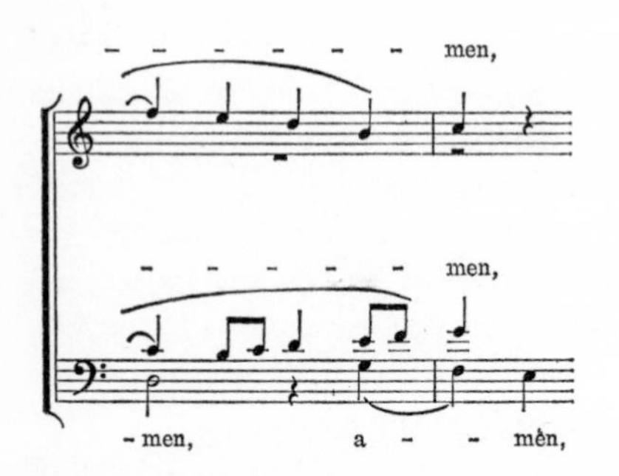

The animated outer sections of the Credo flank an intimate Adagio which emphasizes with particular poignancy the words 'et homo factus est' and 'crucifixus'. The Phrygian close of the Kyrie is reiterated at the close of the whole work in a richer and transcended form, in the final 'dona nobis pacem'. This plea for peace sums up the whole ethos of a work in which, as Nowak has said, 'music becomes prayer'.

Many other memorable passages could be discussed at length, such as the rich key-changes that heighten the meaning of the text in the Gloria, the 'et resurrexit' section of the Credo, where the repeated chords rise up like energy reborn, and the cries of 'miserere' in the Agnus Dei which stand like great Gothic arches, but a whole chapter would fail to do justice to this remarkable Mass. It is significant that in this work Bruckner consciously finds the roots of his inspiration in the Renaissance and yet creates music that more than any other work of the 1860s reveals his true personality.

The Cecilian Movement which welcomed the Mass in E minor was founded by Franz Xaver Witt. He strove for the total exclusion of the orchestra from devotional music of the Roman Catholic Church, and so did not approve of Bruckner's Masses in D minor and F minor. Both Bruckner and Liszt ultimately turned aside from the Cecilian Movement because of its extreme Palestrinianism. The E minor Mass is a perfect illustration of how far Bruckner was prepared to go in this direction without sacrificing his personal style. But he did write some strictly modal smaller sacred works including a Phrygian hymn 'Jam lucis' and a Phrygian 'Pange lingua', both of 1868. Witt published the 'Pange lingua' in 1885 but greatly annoyed Bruckner by 'correcting' some of the most poignant dissonances. A Lydian Gradual 'Os justi' dates from 1879, dedicated to another arch-Cecilianist, Ignaz Traumihler of St Florian. Bruckner wrote to him: 'I should be very pleased if you found pleasure in the piece. It is written without sharps and flats, without the chord of the seventh, without a six-four chord and without chordal combinations of four and five simultaneous notes.'

Despite the severity of these restrictions, this motet is profoundly emotional in effect, the contrapuntal main section being introduced by a homophonic passage including antiphonal responses between the male and female voices of the choir, and a plainsong Alleluia closes the work.

The Mass in F minor followed Bruckner's period of personal and professional crisis in 1867 and was completed in the following year. It is his thanksgiving to God for his return to mental and spiritual health. He revised it several times until 1881, when it took on its authentic form. A later revision of 1890–3 was undertaken with Joseph Schalk. Leopold Nowak's edition incorporates changes of orchestration which Bruckner made in 1890–1893, though Robert Haas believed that this version contains many unauthorized changes and his edition is based on the original autograph and the revision of 1881. As in the previous Masses, there are many themes influenced by plainsong, notably the first themes of the Gloria and Credo and the 'Pleni sunt coeli' of the Sanctus. The work opens with a step-wise descending motif of four notes in the strings which is taken up by the voices, the basses having an inversion of the motif. Descending groups of four consecutive notes propel much of the Gloria, and they pervade much of the Agnus Dei. In the 'Christe eleison' soprano and bass soloists join the chorus and a solo violin hovers above with an effect reminiscent of the Benedictus of Beethoven's Missa Solennis. The second Kyrie has a new accompaniment and moves to fresh keys: D flat, followed by a climax on a six-four chord of E major and a final climax, again with soprano and bass soloists in C flat (enharmonic B major) and the chorus turn through C and G flat major back to the home key in the first, and therefore most effective, unaccompanied passage of the Mass—a moment that reappears in Symphony No. 2. Both the Gloria and the Credo, which together form a highly dramatic centrepiece, are in a jubilant C major, close in key and joyful mood to the Te Deum and Psalm 150. Another link with these works occurs in the 'Et resurrexit' section, where an exuberant string motif forms an accompaniment for 101 bars. It is of the same persistent character as the important figures in the Te Deum, Psalm 150 and the sketch of the finale of Symphony No. 9:

The central 'Qui tollis peccata mundi' section of the Gloria is in slower tempo in D minor, and its more contrapuntal character contrasts well with the homophonic outer sections. The Gloria ends with a triumphant double fugue to the words 'In gloria Dei Patris' and 'Amen', and involves multiple *stretti* and inversion. The movement closes with a mighty plagal cadence. The Credo contains some vividly colourful writing, for example the play between *fortissimo* chorus and *pianissimo* soloists at 'Deum de Deo', or the violin, viola and tenor solo parts in the E major 'Et incarnatus'. This movement also ends with a double fugue of astonishing power. Its main subject is derived from the opening theme of the Credo, and the flow of polyphony is punctuated by bold cries of 'Credo! Credo!':

The figure (x) in the Credo theme is an ascending form of the opening four-note motif of the Mass, but this does not become clear until the end of the 'Dona nobis pacem'.

The Sanctus, in F major, quotes the 'Christe' of the opening movement, and the soprano soloist opens the Hosanna in a bright D major. The Benedictus has a seventeen-bar string prelude which shares the thematic material of the first entry of the soloists. The second theme is sung by the bass soloist with answering phrases from the sopranos and altos of the chorus. There is an instrumental link between the A flat major of the Benedictus and the reprise of the Hosanna in D major. The opening string motif of the eight-bar prelude to the Agnus Dei, which contains the descending four-note idea, forms a counterpoint to the choral entry. In the 'Dona nobis pacem' the Kyrie material reappears, and towards the end there is a *fortissimo* statement of the 'Amen' fugue-subject of the Gloria; this is followed by the Credo theme in augmentation, and now the relation of this theme to the opening motif of the Mass is made clear. This descending motif from the first bar of the Kyrie brings Bruckner's greatest symphonic festive Mass to a gentle close.

The F major motet 'Asperges me', of the same year, is an excellent example of how Bruckner can base a work almost entirely on a plainsong outline and yet transform his material with chromatic harmony and melodic inflections. The C major gradual 'Locus iste' of 1869 is magically simple and effective and contains more than a hint of the priests' chorus from *The Magic Flute*. The opening is hauntingly beautiful:

Ex 13

The gradual is in *ABA* form with homophonic outer parts enclosing an imitative central section which has a climax on B major. The return of Ex. 13 is smoothly achieved. The later motets of Bruckner are unjustly neglected and yet none of them presents major problems for a competent choir. An exploration of this little-known aspect of Bruckner's output brings exquisite rewards —there are no rivals to works like 'Tota pulchra es Maria' (1878), 'Christus factus est' (four-part setting, 1884), 'Virga Jesse floruit' (1885) or 'Vexilla regis' (1892) among the output of all Bruckner's contemporaries. 'Ecce sacerdos', with organ and trombones, is the boldest of these works. It is a model example of Bruckner's homophonic choral writing at its finest, his contrapuntal mastery, his use of brass instruments to emphasize the text, his use of material based on plainsong and his extraordinary harmonic daring (e.g. the climactic sequence of unrelated chords at 'Ideo jurejurando'). The work was written to celebrate the thousandth anniversary of the Diocese of Linz in 1885.

There are only two major choral works of the Vienna period. The first of these, the Te Deum, completed in 1886, may justifiably be called Bruckner's greatest choral work. Dedicated to his 'dear Lord', it is a gigantic hymn of praise that sums up the composer's rock-like personal faith. The key is C major for strident arpeggio figures (see Ex. 11) and *tutti* outbursts of brass and chorus that alternate with moments of hushed awe. But there are passages of warmth and beauty which throw these outbursts into splendid relief, such as the two sections in F minor for soloists, 'Tu ergo' and 'Salvum fac'. A solo violin finds voice in these sections and appears in a similar role in the central section of Psalm 150. The various sections of the Te Deum are thematically linked. The soloists prepare for the vast double fugue that ends the work, with 'In te, Domine, speravi', and this is joined by the 'Non confundar in aeternum' theme. The two are then contrapuntally interwoven in a shattering climax that reveals Bruckner's spiritual strength as well as his consummate mastery of technique.

Psalm 150 of 1892, Bruckner's last sacred choral work, shares both the key and the triumphant mood of rapturous exaltation of the Te Deum. Like the earlier work, it uses themes inspired by plainsong and is scored for a full orchestra and chorus, but with only one soprano solo. The Psalm also ends with a complex fugue, which builds up to a victorious peroration. It is, like the Te Deum, a personal statement of faith, 'charged with the grandeur of God'.

14 The symphonies in major keys

Perhaps if Wagner had first perused the score of Bruckner's Fourth Symphony in E flat major, rather than his Third, then the composer's Bayreuth nickname might have been 'Bruckner the Horn', rather than 'The Trumpet'. The horns play a memorable part throughout the symphony, notably at statements of the principal themes of both outer movements and throughout much of the Andante, and not unnaturally they preside over the events of the 'Hunt' Scherzo. This captivating use of the horns, poetically evident at the very outset of the work (see Ex. 2, p. 74) is justification enough for Bruckner's own sub-title to this symphony, 'The Romantic'. It is his only use of a descriptive subtitle and, while it is not inappropriate, it should not mislead the listener into an expectation of any features normally associated with nineteenth-century Romantic ideology.

The opening bars have a warmth, solemn breadth and unhurried dignity, enhanced by the use of major tonality, that instantly mark the first movement as the most perfect yet conceived by Bruckner. For an entire decade all his large-scale works were written in major keys, from the Fourth Symphony, written in 1874, through the Fifth, Sixth and Seventh Symphonies and String Quintet to the *Te Deum* of 1884. This is an especially striking feature when it is recalled that the previous five symphonies and all the major sacred choral works shared minor tonality. The major-key symphonies also share a somewhat less tangible quality, namely a pervading mood of creative confidence. With the Fourth Symphony Bruckner overcame most of the weaknesses which bedevilled the Third, and the very fact that Symphonies 5, 6 and 7 (and also the Quintet and *Te Deum*) were hardly revised at all shows that they sprang from an untroubled and confident state of mind, hardly paralleled at any other point in Bruckner's career. In the light of all this the majestic glow of the opening subject of Symphony No. 4 has all the more wonder, and signals with hushed awe the start of an enchanting sequence of transformations that Ex. 2 will undergo, such as the new harmonic lights that appear from bar 12, the ever-varying accompaniment and counterpoints to the theme (see the openings of the development, bar 193, recapitulation, bar 365, and coda, bar 501) and most powerfully of all when its rhythm is used as a chorale towards the end of the development (bar 305).

This movement is a sonata structure, and can be discussed in sonata terms. In both outer movements of Symphony No. 3 Bruckner was struggling with a new formal conception which ran against the grain of sonata form and which led to serious weaknesses, most importantly the forestalling of the recapitulatory climax with a massive statement of the opening theme in the tonic key in the development. The first movement of Symphony No. 4 does not attempt to solve the specific problems met in No. 3. Rather it seems Bruckner realized that he had more to say within a more orthodox structure before he was ready to wrestle successfully with a new concept. However, even the fairly inexperienced Brucknerite should not expect a sonata movement in the classical sense of the term. The time-scale and breadth of ideas will be different, and the key-relations and development of motifs will be distinctly unclassical. The opening subject is indeed broad—a seventy-four-bar span, of which the second part is a powerful theme in the home key using the mixed Bruckner rhythm. There is no immediate restatement of this material (as there is in the first groups of Symphonies 3, 6, 7 and 8) but instead a grand formal cadence in the dominant of B flat. The obvious nature of this cadential gesture is too great for all but the most unwary listener to expect that Bruckner will actually begin his second subject in the academically 'correct' key of B flat, and the new idea enters in a spontaneous D flat major. In the recapitulation the same relationship of keys is kept —the cadence on the dominant of A flat heralding the second theme in B major (bar 437). The Coda, propelled by *ostinato* quaver figures, is given new harmonic life by the introduction of C minor, an obvious enough key for an E flat major movement, and yet almost entirely avoided for 500 bars until this point.

The Andante is a march, funereal and restrained. Its opening paragraph never strays far from C minor, although C flat major is more than once suggested, and it contains three expansive ideas:

The dotted rhythm (*a*) is an important linking phrase and (B) is a solemn chorale theme. The whole section ends in C major and is followed by a development of (A), with new figures momentarily revealing a vein of suppressed gaiety and moving from C flat major through a wider spectrum of keys. C minor returns for a re-statement of (A) and (C), the latter beginning in

D minor and closing in D major. The Coda in C minor (bar 193) is built up using (A) with new semiquaver figures and reaches a mighty C major climax, which glances once more towards C flat major before relaxing quietly with drum taps and hints of phrases of (B) and (C). The effect of the whole movement is almost statuesque, the quiet dignity of the opening C minor never having been ruffled during the modestly solemn procession.

Over a string *tremolando* hunting horns announce the main idea of the Scherzo. The key is B flat major and the rhythm characteristic:

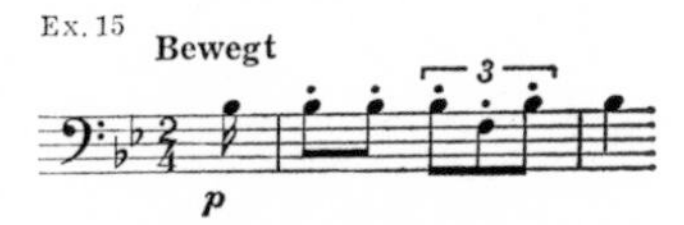

A *crescendo* soon mounts, with dissonances piled up over a tonic pedal. This is resolved unexpectedly by a *fortissimo* phrase in G flat for horns, trombones and tuba, answered brightly by trumpets in B flat major. The Bruckner rhythm continues to predominate in the succeeding string phrase, which answers this outburst with a figure neatly derived from it. A *crescendo* over a dominant pedal in F ensues. The exposition ends with resounding triplet chords for full woodwind, and the development steals in reflectively a semitone higher in G flat major, which is also the key of the Trio.

It can well be argued that Bruckner had written nothing finer than the first three movements of this symphony. Unfortunately the finale runs aground more than once and, as in the previous symphony, he has not yet the skill to refloat it. His stream of thought is about to flow into a broad and magnificent sweep but in this finale a last stretch of rocks and rapids has to be encountered. To stretch the analogy a little further, these rocks and rapids are the vestiges of sonata form which the composer has not yet been able to discard. As in the Third Symphony they impede his natural flow of thought and destroy the momentum of the music. Again the recapitulation is the stumbling point in the movement: it appears as in sonata form and yet its character and the breadth of its conception demand an altogether different treatment, the kind of treatment that Bruckner perfected in Symphonies 5 and 8, works whose finales, although quite different, are a perfect foil to the previous three movements. In the Fourth Symphony finale the weakest element is the second thematic group. This begins promisingly (bar 93) but soon sinks into banality, trite melody and irritatingly repetitive one- and two-bar phrases. Each time this material rears its head it seems more tired and threadbare, particularly throughout the development, which, after a promising start, is interrupted by the second-group material dressed up as a chorale.

The weakness of this section is all the more regrettable in view of the magnificent and totally different opening subject-matter. The movement begins mysteriously in B flat minor over an *ostinato*, and a *crescendo* blazes up with the rhythm of the scherzo playing an important part and spills over into the home key with the main subject:

The Bruckner rhythm appears in crotchet and minim values in this theme, and the figure (x) becomes one of the most important and effective elements in succeeding *tutti* passages. Whenever the mood of this opening subject returns Bruckner rivets the attention, despite the lapses that occur in between, and the Coda particularly is engineered with infallible logic and finality. Had the mood of the second subject permeated the coda then the result might have been a bombastic peroration. Instead there is a *crescendo* of great dignity and a final blaze of E flat major with trombones and tuba reiterating the rhythm of Ex. 2 (p. 74). The whole symphony is unified not only by several recollections of the rhythm of the opening theme (and its literal quotation at bar 79 of the finale) but also by subtle thematic integration such as the use of the Bruckner rhythm in the first, third and fourth movements, the drop of the fifth in the first themes of the first two movements and similar treatments of the fourth and fifth in the Scherzo. (There is also a similarity of mood between passages of the Andante and the Finale—compare bars 101 fol. of the Andante with bars 269 fol. of the Finale.)

Thematic unity is also a feature of Symphony No. 5 in B flat major, but the techniques employed in its finale are strikingly different from those in any other Bruckner symphony and the movement is so significant that it demands a fairly detailed thematic analysis. The opening section consists of reminiscences of the previous movements, but while these might outwardly suggest the influence of Beethoven's Ninth, the effect and purpose of the thematic recollections are quite different. First to appear is the growing string counterpoint over a *pizzicato* bass from the slow introduction to the opening movement, with the significant addition of a falling octave-figure from the clarinet. There is a pause and the clarinet octave-figure appears stark and alone, now extended to become the motto figure of the entire movement. Now follows the main theme of the opening movement (appearing exactly as in bars 55 to 62 of the first movement), again with the addition of falling octaves from clarinet followed by trumpet. The motto theme once more appears questioningly and arrestingly, and then the oboe theme that opened the Adagio makes its entry accompanied by the *pizzicato* triplet string figures that linked the Adagio and the Scherzo. Again the motto figure sounds—now on two clarinets—and is taken up by the cellos and basses and extended to form the first fugue subject:

This section is a grand march-like fugal exposition (bars 31–66), the *tutti* dying away on the home dominant and leading to a non-fugal 'second subject' in D flat major. This new group, which is in graceful contrast to the fugal material, flows through brighter keys but also ends on the home dominant (bar 136). A *tutti* follows, based on the motto figure in augmentation and in its original form, with scale figures in the strings which take their cue from the second subject. The exposition ends with a great chorale, stated antiphonally by resounding brass and quiet strings (bar 175):

This final paragraph moves from G flat major to a quiet F major (the home dominant again—a Neapolitan relationship) and after a few moments' reflection on the chorale melody, a second fugal exposition begins with this very theme as subject (bar 223). Soon both fugue-subjects (Exx. 17 and 18) are combined (bar 270) and a massive development ensues in which they are freely interwoven and inverted. The effect is that of a grand and vastly extended symphonic *tutti*. The detailed progress of the two subjects is best left undescribed as it provides a source of constant wonder at every hearing. The climax comes with a mighty statement of the two subjects combined, preceded by a *crescendo* (bar 374)—a moment that has the feel of a recapitulatory climax, but such terminology is redundant in any attempt to map the mighty swing of Bruckner's creative process in this particular movement. The second subject follows, with subtle transformations, in F major. As before, a *tutti* section ensues, but the principal subject of the first movement now joins in to play a conspicuous role. The Coda (bar 496) has a breadth and grandeur which are unparalleled in Bruckner's output. It begins quietly with scale-patterns and the motto figure, soon combined with the theme from the first movement. The climax of the whole movement is achieved when the motto figure appears in augmentation both in its original form and in inversion, and then forms a background to the chorale which blazes forth resplendently in the brass. The main theme of the opening movement ends this finale in which Bruckner seems to link heaven and earth in one immutable visionary span. With it is the final proof of his awakened mastery, and the enemy's jeers are left far, far behind.

Strangely, the Bruckner rhythm plays virtually no part in the Fifth Symphony, whereas it dominated most of the Fourth. In Symphony No. 6 in A major it becomes a driving force which is predominant from the outset (see Ex. 19 overleaf). The metrical complexities caused by this rhythm (including combined statements in different note values) are more marked in the first movement of the Sixth Symphony than in any other work and this may be a factor in the strange neglect that the work has suffered. As with Symphony No. 5, Bruckner never heard a complete performance of it, nor was it published until after his death. His own opinion was: 'The Sixth is the cheekiest'. The rarity of its performance is all the more surprising in view of its bright character and key, and its abundance of warm and memorable themes.

The foreign notes, G natural, B flat and F natural, in Ex. 19

are characteristic Neapolitan elements and they foreshadow several Neapolitan relationships which follow. The theme extends over twenty bars or so, accompanied throughout by the rhythm (*x*), and incorporates an important motif:

There is a *tutti* counterstatement. As the development gathers energy, freely inverted statements of Exx. 19 and 20 reveal the glorious richness of Bruckner's melodic imagination in a particular way unique to this symphony. This development is propelled throughout by the triplet figures which first made their appearance during the third subject of the exposition. Similarly at the end of the movement they flow into the coda (bar 309) and glide alongside serene reflections of Ex. 19. The rhythm (x) returns for the last *tutti* statement, which is a vast plagal cadence based on Ex. 19. A word must be added about the approach to the recapitulation, which in some ways foreshadows the first movement of Symphony No. 8. During the development of Ex. 20 the tempo quickens, and Ex. 19, together with its accompanying rhythmic figure (x), appears in fullest splendour in E flat major —the polar opposite of the home key, A major. Immediately it is restated in G flat, then again in A flat which becomes the home dominant and the whole first subject appears *fff* in the tonic, followed this time by a quiet counterstatement (the opposite procedure to the exposition). This approach to the recapitulation is arresting, dramatic and truly climactic.

Tovey rightly remarked that the F major Adagio of this symphony has 'a high order of solemn beauty'. It is cast in colossal but clear sonata form and is the only example in the symphonies of a sonata structure Adagio. The elegiac oboe addition to the main theme (bar 5) is related to the rhythm of Ex. 20 of the first movement. More significantly it occurs again in the finale (bar 130), in the course of which movement its relation to Ex. 20 becomes clear.

Bruckner's scherzos are by no means all alike: their differences are much more striking than their similarities. The example from Symphony No. 6 inhabits an enchanted world all of its own. The tempo is slower than usual and the key A minor. A captivating feature is Bruckner's avoidance of a root-position tonic chord for the first hundred bars of this Scherzo: A major is only grasped firmly in the final few *tutti* bars. The Trio is a dialogue between *pizzicato* strings, three horns and woodwind. The key is C major, though this seems to be a point for debate: the string chords pointing towards D flat major and the woodwind quoting the main theme of Symphony No. 5 in A flat major, turning it upside down at the last appearance. This Trio is utterly unlike that of any other Bruckner symphony. If the myth of the stereotyped Bruckner symphony still needs exploding, then a comparison between the finales of this symphony and its mighty predecessor is recommended. The Finale is an assertion of A major against its Neapolitan relatives and is crowned in the last bars with an appearance of Ex. 19.

The work which brought to Bruckner the fullest measure of success and the greatest joy in his lifetime was Symphony No. 7 in E major. It was his turning point towards an international reputation. Today it remains the most readily accessible and strikingly beautiful of all his symphonies. Of them all, the Seventh has had the easiest passage and has enjoyed the greatest popularity. Accompanied by a *tremolando* the first theme appears, twenty-one bars long and cast in a series of noble arches:

A key to the drama of the whole first movement is found here in the early insistence (by the ninth bar in fact) of the dominant key, B major. The solemn arpeggio motif (*a*) of the first three bars of Ex. 21 and the figure (*b*) from bars 10 to 11 are elements of distinct importance throughout the movement. There follows a fully scored counterstatement. With the opening of the tranquil second thematic group (bar 51) we are faced with the Toveyan riddle, 'When is a key not a key?' The opening of the second group is *on* but not *in* the dominant. B major is not yet settled, and at this point there has been no clear modulation to it. However, towards the end of the second group (bar 103) a huge crescendo builds up on the dominant of B and so a new and important third theme enters in B minor (see Ex. 4). This moment comes as a great release in tension and the pattern of the drama now becomes clear—it is based on the relationship of the tonic key, E major, and the forthright and more firmly established dominant key of B. The exposition ends in B major with lyrical calm.

The succeeding development of the material can be broadly viewed in several sections. The first is concerned with imitative reflections on Ex. 21 in inversion and the second with the main idea of the second group, also in inversion. The third theme follows in E minor accompanied by its own mirror inversion, enhanced with new counterpoints, and settling on the dominant of C. Now enters a mighty statement of Ex. 21 in the key of C minor with grandly resounding imitations from the brass section. There is a counterstatement in D minor which moves towards A flat major but is forestalled by the return of the theme in the home key of E, a truly wonderful entry after the grim darkness of the C minor statement. The second group enters now in E minor, significantly avoiding the dominant, and the third group, which played the most important role in establishing B in the exposition, now enters in the new and surprising key of G. This is the crucial point of the movement—a skilful, quiet and purposeful avoidance of the establishment of the dominant key. With the Coda comes a solemn and noble climax which fully establishes the home key, and E major shines forth in its own right for the first time since Ex. 21 (*a*) opened the movement.

On 22nd January 1883, three weeks before Wagner's death,

Bruckner began the Adagio. He wrote to Felix Mottl: 'One day I came home and felt very sad. The thought had crossed my mind that before long the Master would die, and then the C sharp minor theme of the Adagio came to me.'

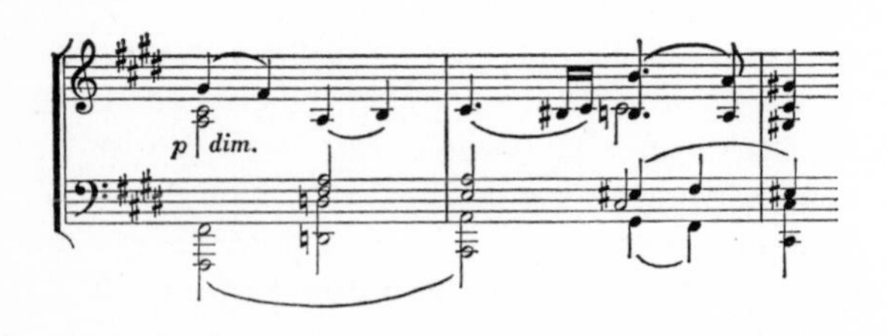

The first phrase of this most solemn theme is stated by a quartet of Wagner tubas—the first occasion on which Bruckner called for these instruments. The impassioned continuation is declaimed by the strings. Ex. 22 is but the opening span of the theme, which is over thirty bars long. The second main theme is in F sharp major. It is set in a faster three-four time, has a characteristic 'off the beat' start, and is truly ravishing:

The span of the movement can be summarized: *ABA¹B¹A² Coda*. The two themes are thus counterstated each in a richly expanded variation (*A¹* and *B¹*). Their respective tempi and distinct orchestration are retained in both of these statements. *A²* becomes the great climax of the movement. The tubas carry the opening theme over new accompaniments, and as the tension mounts the trombones introduce the theme that Bruckner uses in his *Te Deum* at the words 'Non confundar in aeternum', which is treated in sequence. This is a quotation of obvious programmatic significance. At the height of the climax the music is poised on the dominant of the home key, C sharp, only to open on to C major at the crucial moment. This is a most wonderful letting-in of the light, which effectively releases the tension of one of Bruckner's finest crescendos and at the same time reserves the radiant glow of the tonic major for the coda. Bruckner was understandably much affected by the news of Wagner's death, and his reaction found its artistic sublimation in the elevated coda to the movement—sombre music for tubas and horns, ending with a transfigured major version of the opening melody. Bruckner always referred to this passage as 'the funeral music for the Master'.

There has been much discussion of the controversial cymbal clash at the point of climax in this slow movement, which appears in certain editions of the score. I would agree with Dr Robert Simpson's apt comment that Bruckner's climax is quite noble enough to withstand the cymbal crash here, and so it is not a very serious point to dispute. But for the record it ought to be stated that the idea was not Bruckner's own, and this is revealed in a letter of Joseph Schalk to his brother Franz of 10th January 1885:

> Recently I went with Löwe over the score of the Seventh Symphony with regard to some changes and emendations. . . . Perhaps you do not know that Nikisch has insisted on the acceptance of our desired cymbal clash in the Adagio, as also on triangle and timpani, which pleases us immensely.

The funereal serenity of the Adagio gives way to two movements of the most impassioned confidence and exultation that Bruckner ever wrote. The A minor Scherzo has a wild and playful joy that at moments anticipates Mahler and even Elgar. The section is cast in orthodox sonata form but all the elements of the design are stated in the first twelve bars. Throughout the movement rapid shifts from key to key should be observed, and the development section is rich in *stretti*, inversions and many intricate contrapuntal combinations of the several motifs of the movement. The F major Trio, introduced by a rhythm from the Scherzo on the drum, is cast in binary form. A straightforward pastoral melody pervades it, which is inverted at the beginning of the second section. The key of the Trio has a fresh and appealing quality, as it was nowhere found in the Scherzo and only treated as a sequential passing key in the earlier movements. Similarly the A minor of the Scherzo was avoided in the Adagio, and C sharp minor in turn was not used before the slow movement despite its close relation to the home key of E.

The opening *arpeggio* theme of the Finale is closely related to the opening of the first movement, and at the end of the symphony both themes merge together. The fourth movement is one of grand jubilation, uniting gaiety and grandeur and tackling a new formal conception (only most tentatively related to sonata form) in a way that is different from all the other finales. Once again the essential drama of the music is a tonal struggle, in this case between E major and A flat major. The whole structure is like an advance towards an inevitable E major. As usual the key to this appears at the very outset: the first theme opens in E major and closes with a firm cadence in A flat. This distinctive cadential figure always has the effect of pulling the music rapidly from one key to another. The second subject is a chorale-like theme for strings with *pizzicato* bass. The third principal idea is a striding dramatic theme for full orchestra in unison, not far removed from the opening motif of the movement in outline. The splendid effect of its dotted rhythms marching upwards in the brass recalls the magnificence of the finale of the Fifth Symphony.

15 The Eighth and Ninth Symphonies

The brightest fortunes of Bruckner's last years were the result of the tremendous success of the Seventh Symphony. Its successor, Symphony No. 8 in C minor, which he regarded as his finest work, caused him the greatest emotional strain of his whole career.

In 1885 Hermann Levi had triumphed with the première of the Seventh Symphony in Munich, which Bruckner attended. He promised to devote his energy to the further establishment of Bruckner's fame, and the delighted composer accepted the conductor as his friend and 'artistic father' and proceeded with his next symphony. The Eighth is a far bigger and more complex work than any of its predecessors: when Levi received the score in 1887 he rejected it in bewilderment (see Chapter 6). The shock of his artistic father's reaction plunged Bruckner into an intensive revision of the score, which he completed in 1890. Thus there are two versions of the score, the 1887 original and the 1890 revision. There are many radical differences between these two versions which deserve comment, but first the more familiar version must be examined, that is the 1890 revision. (It must be remembered that Haas incorporated certain elements of the original 1887 version of the work in his edition of the 1890 score. He restored ten bars of the Adagio, and thirty-eight of the finale which Bruckner had simply excised, most probably as a result of Joseph Schalk's persuasion. These restorations are quite justifiable, and because of them Haas has given us a score that makes far more musical sense and has a better formal balance.)

Ambiguous tonality characterizes the opening of the symphony. A violin *tremolando* on F forms the background to the opening theme in the lower strings. It instantly conveys the impression of a first unit reaching out over what must surely be a mighty span:

This is a daring opening for a symphony in C minor. In fact it begins in what would appear to be B flat minor and turns dramatically to C only at its close. These two keys, B flat minor and C minor, are of crucial significance in the overall structure. Indeed the whole structure can be legitimately viewed as a duel between them. The dotted rhythm of the first three bars of the theme is identical to the rhythm of the opening of Beethoven's Ninth, but both its character and the direction of its harmonies are utterly different. The figure (*c*) at the end of the first phrase is found as a cadence figure at various important points in the symphony, particularly at the end of the first movement, in modified form in the coda of the Adagio, and at the close of the entire work where it is reiterated in a C major transformation. The tiny figure (*a*) also plays its own part, often in inversion, and appearing in tense and sinister repetitions. By bar 8, Ex. 24(*b*) has grown into a new variant, and the further continuation of the theme shows it growing organically into new shapes. This process is characteristic of the motivic development that all the important themes of the work undergo. As the *tremolando* rises in chromatic steps, the lower strings embrace the Bruckner rhythm. This rhythm is taken up by all the strings and inverted, and the whole opening idea cadences fleetingly in the home key. Without any pause a *fortissimo* counterstatement ensues.

Imitative reflections on the Bruckner-rhythm motif extend the close of the counterstatement and lead into the second-subject group (bar 51), which is derived from this very motif. Thus the first- and second-subject groups are organically linked. During the course of the second thematic section the triplet figures of the Bruckner rhythm are to the fore, and so another link is formed, this time to the third-subject group (bar 97), which is permeated throughout by triplet rhythms. In his early minor-key symphonies (and it should be recalled that this is the composer's third C minor symphony) Bruckner modulated to the relative major for his second subject. In the first movement of the Eighth the second subject is in G major, and the relative major, E flat major, is attained only at the very end of the exposition where it is celebrated by a pæan of fanfares (bar 125). This latest idea—the arpeggio fanfare—can be discerned throughout the work as well (notably in the Finale at bars 11 and 25, and in the coda of the Finale after bar 726).

The masterly central section of the movement is one of the most impressive passages in Bruckner's entire output. Broadly viewed, the E flat fanfare passage is followed by a return of the opening theme and the 'development' section enters almost imperceptibly. Inversions of Ex. 24 are the first points of discussion, followed by an appearance of the inverted second subject, set in new and richer tonalities. Then the music settles on the dominant of the home key. This moment is easily recognized. The figure (*a*) of Ex. 24 is reiterated in the bass while the Bruckner-rhythm motif ascends inexorably in the upper strings. The expectation of a recapitulation in the home key is aroused by this passage, but then figure (*a*) begins to climb upwards ominously in the bass until it becomes fixed on the dominant of B flat minor—the other element in this great combat of keys. And so the opening idea (in augmentation) is recapitulated in a massive statement in B flat minor, which lifts into C major, with the addition of the Bruckner-rhythm motif in augmentation above. Eight horns celebrate with exuberant dotted rhythms. Then there is a sudden shift into D flat minor and the theme is repeated again, this time opening on E flat major. A third statement follows in the next breath in F minor, which now ends in C minor and the blaze of sound is cut off, leaving a single flute trailing down and the cellos and basses reiterating figure (*c*) with a disconsolate air. The trumpets announce the rhythm of the opening theme on a monotone of C. The figure (*c*) is then taken up and used in a swirling passage which leads to a recapitulation of the entire opening theme in C minor, beginning quietly and almost imperceptibly in the oboe (bar 282). This entirely original concept of recapitulation in the form of three huge tonal steps leading to a quiet thematic restatement is engineered in a way that significantly ensures that the home key is not firmly achieved. Thus the tension of the tonal struggle is prolonged.

The C minor Coda is music of profound tragedy. At the height of an overwhelming climax which follows the recapitulation of the third subject group, horns and trumpets repeat the rhythm of Ex. 24 on a stark monotone of C and continue this for four bars after the rest of the orchestra breaks off. Bruckner referred to this moment as 'the annunciation of death'. Drum rolls and shattered fragments (firstly of phrase (*b*) of Ex. 24) follow, and finally phrase (*c*) is repeated over and over again until the movement reaches its quiet close. This last series of repeated phrases of (*a*) was referred to as the *Totenuhr* by Bruckner. A man is dying in a room, but a clock in the room ticks on even when his life has passed away.

The motions of a turbulent spirit that overshadow the first movement are released with elemental freedom and boundless energy in the Scherzo, where two combined one-bar phrases are ecstatically repeated. The prevailing keys are C minor and

E flat major, and in the final nine bars C major. The Trio (cast like the Scherzo in sonata form) employs harps: their first entry at bar 37 with horns and *pizzicato* strings is thoroughly Austrian in character.

Superfically, the Finale has much in common with the first movement, particularly the tonal ambiguity of its opening bars: the dotted rhythm of the first subject, the character of the second group (bar 69), the E flat minor double-unison structure of the third subject (bar 83) and the subsequent establishment of the relative major (E flat) after much suspense. But the specific characters of each of the combined elements—melody, rhythm, harmony and orchestration—are so different that the effect is rather akin to the sensation of experiencing a beclouded and turbulent night that gives way to a lustrous dawn.

Every symphony of Bruckner's is a structure of imposing size and variety, but none of them culminates in a unitary span of the magnificence achieved in No. 8. The culmination of this unitary span is the combination of themes from all four movements in an exultant celebration of the tonic major (bar 735):

It is not contrapuntal ingenuity that dazzles us here, but rather the power, logic and inevitability of this final fusion, cast in the simplicity of a C major chord. The symphony which caused Bruckner the greatest personal anxiety thus represents the very essence of achievement. Its content is of aspiration and struggle towards symphonic unity on an unparalleled scale.

To the listener who is well acquainted with the 1890 score

an examination of how it differs from the original of 1887 will bring many surprises. These differences provide a fascinating insight into the mind of a great artist engaged in totally recasting his original creative conception. The score and parts of the original version were issued in April 1973 in an edition by Nowak, and the version was first performed by the Bournemouth Symphony Orchestra under Hans-Hubert Schönzeler in a B.B.C. broadcast the following September. The original score is inferior in a great many aspects to the final version, and in a sense Levi's rejection (whatever his reasons for it were) did Bruckner a good turn in the long run. The differences are so many that it is far beyond the scope of this chapter to mention more than an important handful of them, but they apply in every movement to every aspect—melody, rhythm, harmony and orchestration.

Instantly striking is the re-orchestration. The 1887 score employed two-part woodwind as opposed to the three-part of the revision. (So much for the myth of Bruckner's dependence on huge orchestral forces.) The four Wagner tubas are much busier in the opening movement in the original version, while the harps disappear from the Trio of the Scherzo, and only one harp is called for in the Adagio, as opposed to the 'three if possible' in the revised score. The Adagio asks for piccolo in the original version and the climax is certainly enhanced by its employment. This is the only instance of Bruckner ever scoring for piccolo. The climax of the original Adagio also contrives to contain six cymbal clashes as opposed to the two in the revision.

The differences of form and tonality between the two scores are the most significant of all and reveal most clearly the benefits of the revision. They are apparent from the outset. It will be recalled that this symphony, in C minor, begins in fact in B flat minor and only reaches the home key at the end of its dramatic first thematic phrase. In the familiar revised version a clarinet figure reinforces C minor when it is achieved, thus confirming the tonality (see Ex. 24). In the original score this figure does not appear. A more important alteration to the first movement is the total overhauling of the approach to the recapitulation, the recapitulation itself and the counterstatement of the opening theme in the recapitulation. This entire central section is vastly superior in the revised score, the original revealing that Bruckner had not properly worked out his ideas, and the sense of the conflict of keys is missing in the earlier score, where the logic of the tonality is lost and the orchestration much less effective. The whole passage benefits in the revision by being shortened. The most noticeable difference in the opening movement, however, is the Coda. The revised version ends tragically and quietly with repetitions of Ex. 24(*c*), and is the only outer movement of all Bruckner's symphonies not to end *fortissimo*. The original, on the other hand, continues after a pause for another thirty bars with a *tutti* peroration which is based on a double augmentation of Ex. 24, passing from B flat minor (harmonized as G flat major) to a triumphant C major. The passage is very effective, but despite this Bruckner was right to discard it, as it forestalls the C major ending of the symphony and thus weakens the overall tonal pattern.

The original Scherzo and Finale are essentially the same as in the revision (aside from countless tiny alterations), except that they were both originally longer. The Scherzo of the original is inferior in a number of small details and is even more obsessed with the principal motif. The Finale of the original contained brass lines at the opening of the Coda and delightful *pianissimo* trumpet fanfares just before the final C major *tutti*. Both these elements were deleted in the revision. The close of the whole symphony differs also in that the great unison statement of the motif derived from Ex. 24(*c*) is missing in the original.

A further word should be said about the Trio of the second movement and the Adagio, both of which were considerably altered. The entire first theme of the Trio is quite different in the original, the important triplet fanfares for trumpets appear as duplets and many other details are strangely different. The climax of the Adagio is longer, orchestrated differently and considerably inferior in the earlier version, but its most striking feature is that the climax comes in C major as opposed to E flat major. There are several possible explanations of this important change. Bruckner may have felt that he should not have his climax in the same key as the Adagio of his previous symphony (the Adagio of No. 7 also culminates in C at its climax). More important, it would seem that he felt (as with the coda to the first movement) that C major must be avoided and kept out of play until the close of the entire drama.

With Symphony No. 9 in D minor Bruckner's range of expression was widened and the visionary quality of his mature style intensified. The first ninety-six bars of the opening movement contain eight principal ideas. There are more things of heaven and earth in this gigantic statement than were ever dreamt of in any other first-subject group:

The form of the movement clearly shows a pattern of 'Statement, Counterstatement and Coda' which is totally divorced from sonata form. Indeed the solemn and broad scope of the first section indicates that quite a different concept lies ahead. The second principal section of the Statement is a slower theme beginning in A major (bar 97), and the third section consists of two main ideas in Moderato tempo (the first beginning in D minor, bar 167, and the second beginning in G flat major, bar 191).

The Counterstatement (bar 227) begins with *stretti* treatments of Ex. 26(A) followed by a glowing appearance of (B). Then (A) and (C) are treated in combination, leading to a still grander appearance of (B). There is a pause and the second idea from the third section enters with *pizzicato* accompaniment. The first-section material continues after this, first with (C), joined shortly by (D) and (E) together. An *accelerando* and *crescendo* lead to the climax of the Counterstatement—a D minor *fff* statement of (F), which proceeds to step forward in new lights and through a series of massive tonal shifts. The second and third sections are in due turn counterstated (bars 421 and 459 respectively) and the Coda (bar 517) returns to ideas from Ex. 26, namely fragments of (B) and (F) and a statement in augmentation of (G) which has not been heard since the original Statement.

The above is the broadest survey of this colossal structure and it takes little or no account of either tonality or the character and interrelationships of themes. It should be stressed that both the Counterstatement and Coda represent one continuous and constant process of development.

Foremost amongst the very apparent features of the Ninth Symphony is its advanced harmonic language. The end of the first movement is a clear example of forthright dissonance—a grinding of simultaneous tonic and flat supertonic harmony. In the strangely troubled world of the D minor Scherzo one particular and unmistakable discord is in evidence in one form or or another throughout the entire movement, while in the spectral Trio 'on horror's head horrors accumulate'. The harmony is at times scarcely definable, for example at the opening of the E major Adagio which has already been mentioned (see Ex. 1, p. 70). The wide leap of the ninth at the outset of the Adagio points forward to Schoenberg, while other ecstatic melodic leaps during the same movement anticipate Mahler.

The unfinished finale occupied Bruckner for the last two years of his life. There exist no fewer than six variants of the movement in sketched full score. These sketches show that the finale was planned on a scale more ambitious than that of the Eighth Symphony or even of the Fifth. Alfred Orel's published edition of the sketches reveals, at least in outline, a gigantic structure consisting of an exposition followed by a development combining a fugue with a recapitulation of the second-subject group. Thus the characteristic tendency of Bruckner's late years towards telescoping development and recapitulation can be observed. But the movement is incomplete and is not completable. Much detail of the inner parts, the sense of coherent continuity and the entire Coda are missing, and none but the composer himself could supply such elements. Bruckner simply did not live long enough to envisage this finale as a truly unified entity. What remains is a torso representing the composer's faithfully recorded final visions; visions which were abruptly ended and not left to the world in a tangible enough form to allow performance or even speculative completion.

It is, however, no mean fragment. Four hundred bars or so in length, the complete sketches do permit a fairly deep insight into Bruckner's creative mind. The mood of the opening is nervous and mysterious, fascinatingly ambiguous and astringent in its harmony. Later on a more assertive chorale theme appears which becomes fused with a motif from the *Te Deum.* This appearance of the opening figuration of the *Te Deum* is entirely in keeping with Bruckner's habit of quotation from his sacred choral works (as seen in Symphonies 0, 2, 3, 7 and the Adagio of No. 9). It has been quite erroneously assumed, however, that he was at this point writing a transition to lead into the earlier work, thus providing the symphony with a choral finale. Such a view is untenable as the dying composer can only have suggested the substitution of the *Te Deum* as a finale as a very desperate solution. The unrelated keys of the two works, and the fact that the appearance of the *Te Deum* motif can be viewed as an entirely characteristic and symbolic programmatic quotation put the idea of appending the *Te Deum* to this symphony beyond the bounds of likelihood. This unjustifiable coupling of the two works was in fact perpetrated by Ferdinand Löwe at the first performance on 11th February 1903, allegedly in accordance with the wishes of the late composer, and others followed his example. Indeed the very existence of an independent finale was tacitly ignored for about three decades until Orel's publication of Bruckner's incomplete 'song of praise to our Lord'.

During Bruckner's Linz years his friend Moritz von Mayfeld dedicated a poem to him, the first and last lines of which were used as a couplet and inscribed upon the first laurel wreath awarded to the composer:

> Art had its beginning in God—
> And so it must lead back to God.

This is the simple motto which accompanied Bruckner throughout every stage of his art. It is the credo that gave him the purpose to fight mental and physical strains until the last morning of his life when the flame flickered out upon the movement that stands as a symbolic last statement of one 'whom death could not daunt'.

Appendices

Appendix A Calendar

Figures in brackets denote the age reached by the person mentioned during the year in question

YEAR	AGE	LIFE	CONTEMPORARY MUSICIANS
1824		Joseph Anton Bruckner born, Sept. 4, at Ansfelden in Upper Austria, son of Anton Bruckner senior (1791–1837), schoolmaster, and his wife Theresa, *née* Helm (1801–1860), eldest of eleven children, five of whom survived infancy.	Cornelius born, Dec. 24; Reinecke born, June 23; Smetana born, March 2. Abt aged 5; Adam 21; Alkan 11; Auber 42; Beethoven 54; Bellini 23; Sterndale Bennett 8; Berlioz 21; Berwald 28; Cherubini 64; Chopin 14; Czerny 33; Dargomizhsky 11; Donizetti 27; Field 42; Franc 2; Franz 9; Glinka 20; Gossec 90; Gounod 6; Halévy 25; Hummel 46; Kalkbrenner 39; Kuhlau 38; Lalo 1; Liszt 13; Loewe 28; Marschner 29; Mendelssohn 15; Meyerbeer 33; Offenbach 5; Paganini 42; Raff 2; Reicha 54; Rossini 32; Salieri 74; Schubert 27; Schumann 14; Sechter 36; Spohr 40; Spontini 50; Johann Strauss (I) 20; Verdi 11; Vieuxtemps 4;

YEAR	AGE	LIFE	CONTEMPORARY MUSICIANS
			Wagner 11; Weber 38; Zelter 66.
1825	1		Hanslick born, Sept. 11; Salieri (75) dies, May 7; Johann Strauss II born, Oct. 25.
1826	2		Weber (40) dies, June 4–5.
1827	3		Beethoven (57) dies, Mar. 26.
1828	4		Schubert (31) dies, Nov. 19.
1829	5	Shows keen interest in music and is encouraged by his father, who gives him his first lessons.	Gossec (95) dies, Feb. 16; Anton Rubinstein born, Nov. 28.
1830	6		Bülow born, Jan. 8.
1831	7		Joachim born, June 28.
1832	8		Clementi (80) dies, Mar. 10; Kuhlau (46) dies, Mar. 12; Zelter (74) dies, May 15.
1833	9	J. B. Weiss (1813–50) acts as godfather at Bruckner's confirmation.	Borodin born, Nov. 12; Brahms born, May 7.
1834	10	Already deputizing for his father at the church organ.	Reubke born, Mar. 23.
1835	11	Moves in the spring to Hörsching, near Linz, and his education continues under Weiss. Hears sacred music of Haydn and Mozart.	Bellini (34) dies, Sept. 24; Cui born, Jan. 18; Saint-Saëns born, Oct. 9.
1836	12	In December, returns to Ansfelden and performs some of the duties of his father, who is seriously ill.	Delibes born, Feb. 21; Reicha (66) dies, May 28.

YEAR	AGE	LIFE	CONTEMPORARY MUSICIANS
1837	13	Father dies, June 7. Accepted as a choirboy at Stift St Florian although his voice is nearly broken. General education continues with organ lessons from Kattinger, violin lessons from Gruber and figured-bass lessons from Bogner. A number of small choral and organ works already composed.	Balakirev born, Jan. 12; Field (55) dies, Jan. 11; Hummel (59) dies, Oct. 17.
1838	14		Bizet born, Oct. 25; Bruch born, Jan. 6.
1839	15		Mussorgsky born, Mar. 21; Rheinberger born, Mar. 17.
1840	16	Decides on a teaching career, passes entrance examination for the teacher-training college in Linz, Oct. 1, and begins the 10-month course. Studies under J. N. A. Dürrnberger, copying fugues by Bach and Albrechtsberger. Hears symphonies by Mozart and Beethoven.	Paganini (58) dies, May 27; Tchaikovsky born, May 7.
1841	17	Passes final exam in Linz, July 30, and becomes a qualified assistant teacher. In October is appointed to a school at Windhaag, near Freystadt (Upper Austria).	Chabrier born, Jan. 18; Dvořák born, Sept. 8.
1842	18	Suffers much hardship in	Cherubini (82) dies, Mar.

YEAR	AGE	LIFE	CONTEMPORARY MUSICIANS
		Windhaag, having to perform menial duties. Plays second fiddle in a band at village entertainments. Composes a small Mass in C.	15; Massenet born, May 12; Sullivan born, May 13.
1843	19	Transferred to Kronstorf, a smaller village between Enns and Steyr, Jan. 23, as a result of complaints about him by his superior at Windhaag, Fuchs. A happier time ensues, and musical studies continue under L. E. von Zenetti of Enns, including further study of Bach.	Grieg born, June 15.
1844	20	Composes a Mass for Maundy Thursday.	Rimsky-Korsakov born, Mar. 18.
1845	21	Passes his second teaching examination, May 29, with great success. Becomes notable as an improvisator at the organ. Appointed assistant teacher at St Florian, Sept. 25.	Fauré born, May 13; Widor born, Feb. 24.
1846	22	Composition of small choral works continues.	
1847	23	Greatly impressed on hearing Mendelssohn's *St Paul* in Linz.	Mendelssohn (38) dies, Nov. 4.
1848	24	Enrols temporarily in the National Guard as a result of the 1848 revolutions. Appointed provisional organist at St Florian.	Donizetti (51) dies, Apr. 8; Duparc born, Jan. 21; Parry born, Feb. 27.

YEAR	AGE	LIFE	CONTEMPORARY MUSICIANS
1849	25	Completes his first notable work, Requiem in D minor, first performed at St Florian, Mar. 13.	Chopin (39) dies, Oct. 17; Kalkbrenner (64) dies, June 10; Johann Strauss I (45) dies, Sept. 25.
1850	26	Studies Latin, and begins two-year course to improve his educational qualifications.	
1851	27	Works as a voluntary clerk in a local court of law. Visits Assmayer in Vienna.	d'Indy born, Mar. 27; Spontini (77) dies, Jan. 14.
1852	28	Composes Magnificat, Psalm 114 and Psalm 22.	Stanford born, Sept. 30.
1853	29		
1854	30	Composes Missa Solemnis in B flat minor, first performed St Florian, Sept. 14, with great success. Passes an organ examination, Oct. 9, with Assmayer, Sechter and Preyer as examiners.	Humperdinck born, Sept. 1; Janáček born, July 3.
1855	31	Passes examination in Linz, Jan. 25–6, qualifying him as a high-school teacher. Robert Führer visits St Florian, April, and gives him a splendid testimonial. Bruckner visits Sechter in Vienna and becomes his pupil, July. The Linz Cathedral organist, Wenzel Pranghofer, dies, and Bruckner distinguishes himself at	Liadov born, May 11.

YEAR	AGE	LIFE	CONTEMPORARY MUSICIANS
		the preliminary examination of candidates, Nov. 13.	
1856	32	Appointed organist at Linz Cathedral, at final audition, Jan. 25. Becomes involved in many activities, receives tuition by post from Sechter, and spends each Lent and Advent with him. Virtually gives up composition for five years.	Adam (53) dies, May 3; Schumann (46) dies, July 29.
1857	33		Czerny (66) dies, July 15; Elgar born, June 2; Glinka (53) dies, Feb. 15.
1858	34	Passes exam in harmony, figured bass and organ playing, July 10.	Leoncavallo born, Mar. 8; Puccini born, June 22; Reubke (24) dies, June 3.
1859	35	Passes elementary counterpoint, Aug. 12.	Spohr (75) dies, Oct. 22.
1860	36	Passes advanced counterpoint, Apr. 3. Bruckner's mother dies. Appointed conductor of the *Liedertafel 'Frohsinn'*, Nov.	Albéniz born, May 29; Mahler born, July 7; Paderwiski born, Nov. 6; Rezniček born, May 4; Wolf born, Mar. 13.
1861	37	Passes canon and fugue, Mar. 26, concluding his studies with Sechter. Composes a fine 7-part Ave Maria, May 12. Resigns from *Liedertafel*, Sept. Commences studies of form and orchestration with Kitzler. Passes an organ examination at the	Arensky born, Aug. 11; Marschner (66) dies, Dec. 14.

YEAR	AGE	LIFE	CONTEMPORARY MUSICIANS
		Piaristenkirche, Vienna, and concludes with a magnificent improvisation, Nov. 22. Psalm 146 and 'Afferentur regi' first performed at St Florian, Dec. 14.	
1862	38	Composes String Quartet, March in D minor, and 3 pieces for orchestra. Is introduced to the music of Wagner and sees *Tannhäuser*.	Debussy born, Aug. 22; Delius born, Jan. 29; Halévy (63) dies, Mar. 17.
1863	39	Composes Overture in G minor, Symphony in F minor and 'Germanenzug'. Meets Lachner in Munich, Sept.	Mascagni born, Dec. 7.
1864	40	Completes Symphony No. 0. Composes Mass in D minor, completed Sept. 29 and first performed at Linz, Nov. 20.	d'Albert born, Apr. 10; Grechaninov born Oct. 25; Meyerbeer (73) dies, May 2; Richard Strauss born, June 11.
1865	41	Begins Symphony No. 1. Meets Wagner, Bülow and Rubinstein and hears *Tristan und Isolde* in Munich, May. Meets Berlioz in Vienna and Liszt in Pest.	Dukas born, Oct. 1; Glazunov born, Aug. 10; Nielsen born, Oct. 2; Sibelius born, Dec. 8.
1866	42	His sister 'Nani' joins him in Linz. Hears Beethoven's Ninth for first time. Completes Symphony No. 1, and on Nov. 25 completes Mass in E minor. At end	Busoni born, Apr. 1; Satie born, Mar. 17.

YEAR	AGE	LIFE	CONTEMPORARY MUSICIANS
		of year suffers severe depression and a total nervous collapse.	
1867	43	Enters a sanatorium for three months, May 8 to Aug. 8. Applies to Hofkapelle and Vienna University for positions, unsuccessfully. Begins Mass in F minor (for which he has already made sketches), Sept. 14.	Granados born, July 29; Koechlin born, Nov. 27; Sechter (79) dies, Sept. 10.
1868	44	Re-appointed conductor of Linz *Liedertafel*. Composes motets, including 'Pange lingua' and 'Inveni David'. Conducts the first performance of the finale of *Die Meistersinger* in Linz, Apr. 4 and first performance of Symphony No. 1 in Linz, May 9. Is persuaded by Herbeck to accept a professorship at the Vienna Conservatorium in succession to Sechter. Moves to Vienna. Completes Mass in F minor, Sept. 9. Begins teaching in Vienna, Oct. 1.	Bantock born, Aug. 7; Berwald (72) dies, Apr. 3; Rossini (76) dies, Nov. 15.
1869	45	Revises Symphony No. 0, Jan. 24 to Sept. 12. Visits France, giving distinguished recitals at Nancy and at Notre Dame, Paris, April–May. Mass in	Berlioz (66) dies, Mar. 8; Dargomizhsky (56) dies, Jan. 17; Loewe (73) dies Apr. 20; Pfitzner born, May 5; Roussel born, Apr. 5.

YEAR	AGE	LIFE	CONTEMPORARY MUSICIANS
		E minor first performed, Linz, Sept. 25. Composes 'Locus iste'. Vienna Philharmonic Orchestra reject Symphony No. 1.	
1870	46	His sister 'Nani' dies. Appointed teacher at St Anna teacher-training college.	Lehár born, Apr. 30.
1871	47	Visits London to give recitals at the Albert Hall and Crystal Palace and is praised for his improvisations, Aug. Returns to Vienna to face a disciplinary action at the College of St Anna. Begins Symphony No. 2 and makes a sketch of 67 bars for a Symphony in B flat major.	Auber (89) dies, May 12.
1872	48	Conducts first performance of Mass in F minor, June 16. Completes Symphony No. 2, Sept. 11, and it is rejected by the Vienna Philharmonic.	Scriabin born, Jan. 4; Vaughan Williams born, Oct. 12.
1873	49	Composes Symphony No. 3, completed Dec. 31. Visits Marienbad, Karlsbad and Bayreuth. Again meets Wagner who accepts dedication of Symphony No. 3. Conducts first performance of Symphony No. 2, Vienna, Oct. 26.	Rakhmaninov born, Apr. 1; Reger born, Mar. 19.
1874	50	Composes Symphony No.	Cornelius (50) dies, Oct.

YEAR	AGE	LIFE	CONTEMPORARY MUSICIANS
		4, completed Nov. 22. Makes several applications to Vienna University for a lectureship but is opposed by Hanslick. Loses his position at the College of St Anna and worries about his financial prospects. Symphony No. 3 revised, and rejected by the Vienna Philharmonic.	26; Holst born, Sept. 21; Ives born, Oct. 20; Franz Schmidt born, Dec. 22; Schoenberg born, Sept. 13.
1875	51	Begins Symphony No. 5, Feb. 14. Sketches 18 bars of a Requiem in D minor, Sept. Appointed lecturer in harmony and counterpoint at Vienna University, July.	Sterndale Bennett (59) dies, Feb. 1; Bizet (37) dies, June 3; Coleridge-Taylor born, Aug. 15; Glière born, Jan. 11; Ravel born, Mar. 7; Tovey born, July 17.
1876	52	Conducts performance of Symphony No. 2, Vienna, Feb. 20, and revises it, making some cuts. Completes first draft of Symphony No. 5, May 16, and commences revising both it and Symphony No. 3. Revises the 3 great Masses. Attends the first 'Ring' cycle at Bayreuth.	Havergal Brian born, Jan. 29; Falla born, Nov. 23; Schelling born, July 26.
1877	53	Moves to a new flat. Completes Symphony No. 5, Aug. Conducts disastrous first performance of Symphony No. 3, but Rättig publishes it and Mahler, with whom Bruckner be-	Dohnányi born, July 27; Karg-Elert born, Nov. 21.

YEAR	AGE	LIFE	CONTEMPORARY MUSICIANS
		comes friendly, helps make a piano duet reduction of it.	
1878	54	Begins a thorough revision of Symphony No. 4. Further revision of Symphonies 3 and 5. Appointed full member of Hofkapelle where he has worked as honorary organist - designate since 1868. Composes 'Tota pulchra es Maria' and begins String Quintet.	Boughton born, Jan, 23; Schreker born, Mar. 23.
1879	55	Composes 'Os justi' and completes String Quintet, July 12. Begins Symphony No. 6, Sept. 24 and writes Intermezzo for string quintet, Dec.	Bridge born, Feb. 26; Ireland born, Aug. 13; Respighi born, July 9; Scott (Cyril) born, Sept. 27.
1880	56	Completes revision of Symphony No. 4, June 5, and continues work on Symphony No. 6. A holiday includes a visit to Oberammergau and a tour of Switzerland.	Bloch born, July 24; Medtner born, Jan. 5; Offenbach (61) dies, Oct. 4.
1881	57	First performance of Symphony No. 4, Feb. 20 (Richter). Begins Te Deum, completes Symphony No. 6, Sept. 3, and begins Symphony No. 7, Sept. 23. First performance of Quintet (incomplete), Nov. 17.	Bartók born, Mar. 25; Miaskovsky born, Apr. 20; Mussorgsky (42) dies, Mar. 28.
1882	58	Continues work on Sym-	Grainger born, July 8;

YEAR	AGE	LIFE	CONTEMPORARY MUSICIANS
		phony No. 7. Visits Bayreuth to hear first performance of *Parsifal* and sees Wagner for the last time.	Kodály born, Dec. 16; Raff (60) dies, June 24–5; Stravinsky born, June 17; Szymanowski born, Oct. 6.
1883	59	Movements 2 and 3 of Symphony No. 6 first performed, Feb. 11 (Jahn). Visits Wagner's grave at Bayreuth, Aug. Completes Symphony No. 7 at St Florian, Sept. 5. Begins final version of Te Deum, Sept. 28.	Bax born, Nov. 6; Casella born, July 25; Wagner (70) dies, Feb. 13; Webern born, Dec. 3.
1884	60	Completes Te Deum, Mar. 7. Visits Prague, and later Bayreuth and Munich. Spends sixtieth birthday quietly in Vöcklabruck. Begins Symphony No. 8. Symphony No. 7 first performed in Leipzig, Dec. 30 (Nikisch) and is a tremendous success.	Smetana (60) dies, May 12.
1885	61	Composes 'Ecce sacerdos' and 'Virga Jesse'. Continues work on Symphony No. 8 (until 1887). First New York performance of Symphony No. 3.	Abt (66) dies, Mar. 31; Berg born, Feb. 9; Butterworth born, July 12; Varèse born, Dec. 22; Wellesz born, Oct. 21.
1886	62	First performance of Te Deum with orchestra, Vienna, Jan. 10 (Richter). First Vienna performance of Symphony No. 7, March (Richter). Awarded	Liszt (75) dies, July 31.

YEAR	AGE	LIFE	CONTEMPORARY MUSICIANS
		Order of Franz-Josef by the Emperor. Visits Bayreuth, and plays at the funeral of Liszt, Aug. 3.	
1887	63	Created an honorary member of the Dutch Maatschappij tot Bevordering der Toonkunst. First London performance of Symphony No. 7, May 23. Completes Symphony No. 8 but Levi's failure to understand it causes a severe deterioration in his nervous condition and a period of 'revision mania' begins with work on Symphony No. 8. Commences Symphony No. 9.	Borodin (54) dies, Feb. 28; Villa-Lobos born, Mar. 5.
1888	64	First 'all Bruckner' concert in Vienna, January (Richter). Revision of phony No. 3 commenced with J. Schalk.	Alkan (75) dies, Mar. 29.
1889	65	Created an honorary member of the Richard Wagner-Verein. Spends a social evening with Brahms. Completes new version of Symphony No. 3 and continues revising Symphony No. 8.	
1890	66	Created honorary member of the Austrian Diet, with a stipend. Chronic catarrh of the larynx aggravates	Franck (68) dies, Nov. 8; F. Martin born, Sept. 15; Martinů born, Dec. 8.

YEAR	AGE	LIFE	CONTEMPORARY MUSICIANS
		his health which is now seriously hampered by dropsy. Retires as organ professor at the Conservatorium. Publications continue during the last years. Completes revision of Symphony No. 8, Mar. 10, and begins a new version of Symphony No. 1, Mar. 12. Plays at the wedding of the Emperor's daughter, Marie Valerie, in Ischl, July 31.	
1891	67	Completes new version of Symphony No. 1, Apr. 18. Attends performance of Te Deum in Berlin, May 31 (Ochs). Visits Bayreuth, Aug. Receives honorary doctorate of Vienna University, Nov. 7. Continues work on Symphony No. 9.	Bliss born, Aug. 2; Delibes (55) dies, Jan. 16; Prokofiev born, Apr. 23.
1892	68	Composes Psalm 150, first performed Nov. 13, 'Das deutsche Lied' and 'Vexilla regis'. Symphony No. 8 first performed, Dec. 18 (Richter).	Franz (77) dies, Oct. 24; Honegger born, Mar. 10; Lalo (69) dies, Apr. 22; Milhaud born, Sept. 4.
1893	69	Created honorary member of the Gesellschaft der Musikfreunde. Composes 'Helgoland', completed Aug. 7. Confined to bed, seriously ill, for much of the year. Makes his will,	Gounod (75) dies, Oct. 18; Tchaikovsky (53) dies Nov. 6.

YEAR	AGE	LIFE	CONTEMPORARY MUSICIANS
		Nov. 10, preserving his 'original scores' 'for future times'. Mental condition deteriorates. Scherzo of Symphony No. 9 completed, Feb. 27, and first movement completed Dec. 23.	
1894	70	Visits Berlin with Hugo Wolf for concerts of their music, Jan., but is too ill to attend the first performance of Symphony No. 5, Graz, Apr. 8 (F. Schalk). Spends seventieth birthday in Steyr and receives many honours. Receives the freedom of the city of Linz, Nov. 15. Resigns from the University. Completes the Adagio of Symphony No. 9, Nov. 30 and presses on with the finale.	Bülow (64) dies, Feb. 12; Chabrier (53) dies, Sept. 13; Anton Rubinstein (65) dies, Nov. 20.
1895	71	Continues work on the finale of Symphony No. 9 despite weakening mental and physical condition. Moves to a gatekeeper's lodge at the Schloss Belvedere, placed at his disposal by the Emperor, July.	Hindemith born, Nov. 16; Orff born, July 10.
1896	72	Attends his last concert, a performance of the Te Deum, Jan. 12. In his last weeks serious depression and a tendency towards	Gerhard born, Sept. 25. Albéniz aged 36; Arensky 35; Balakirev 59; Bantock 28; Bartók 15; Bax 12; Berg 11; Bliss 5; Bloch 16;

YEAR	AGE	LIFE	CONTEMPORARY MUSICIANS
		religious mania set in. On Sunday, Oct. 11, works on the finale of the Symphony in the morning and dies quietly later in the day. Funeral held in the Karlskirche, Vienna, Oct. 14 and his body laid to rest at St Florian.	Boughton 18; Brahms 63; Havergal Brian 20; Bridge 17; Bruch 58; Busoni 30; Butterworth 11; Casella 13; Coleridge-Taylor 21; Cui 61; d'Albert 32; Debussy 34; Delius 34; Dohnányi 19; Dukas 31; Duparc 48; Dvořák 55; Elgar 39; Falla 19; Fauré 51; Glazunov 31; Glière 21; Grainger 14; Granados 29; Grechaninov 31; Grieg 53; Hanslick 71; Hindemith 1; Holst 22; Honegger 4; Humperdinck 42; d'Indy 45; Ireland 17; Ives 21; Janáček 42; Joachim 65; Karg-Elert 18; Kodály 13; Koechlin 28; Leoncavallo 38; Liadov 41; Mahler 36; F. Martin 6; Martinů 5; Mascagni 32; Massenet 54; Medtner 16; Miaskovsky 15; Milhaud 4; Nielsen 31; Orff 1; Paderewski 36; Parry 48; Pfitzner 27; Prokofiev 5; Puccini 38; Rakhmaninov 23; Ravel 21; Reger 23; Respighi 17; Rezniček 36; Rheinberger 57; Rimsky-Korsakov 52; Roussel 27; Saint-Saëns 61; Satie 30; Schelling 20; Schmidt 21; Schoen-

YEAR	AGE	LIFE	CONTEMPORARY MUSICIANS
			berg 22; Schreker 18; Scott (Cyril) 17; Sibelius 30; Scriabin 24; Stanford 44; Johann Strauss II 70; Richard Strauss 32; Stravinsky 14; Sullivan 54; Szymanowsky 14; Tovey 21; Varèse 10; Vaughan Williams 24; Verdi 83; Villa-Lobos 9; Webern 12; Wellesz 10; Widor 52; Wolf 36.

Appendix B Catalogue of works

LARGE-SCALE SACRED WORKS

Mass in C major, for contralto, two horns and organ (*c.* 1842).

Choral Mass for Maundy Thursday in F major, for four-part chorus (1844).

Requiem in D minor, for soloists, chorus, orchestra and organ (1848–1849; revised 1854 and 1894; pub. 1931, ed. Haas, and 1966, ed. Nowak).

Magnificat in B flat major, for soloists, chorus, orchestra and organ (1852).

Psalm 114, for five-part chorus and three trombones (1852).

Psalm 22, for four-part chorus and pianoforte (1852).

Missa Solemnis in B flat minor, for soloists, chorus and orchestra (1854; pub. 1934).

Psalm 146, for soloists, chorus and orchestra (*c.* 1860; pub. 1971).

Psalm 112, for double chorus and orchestra (incomplete) (1863; completed edition pub. 1926, ed. Wöss).

Mass in D minor, for soloists, chorus, orchestra and organ (1864; revised 1876 and 1881; pub. 1892, and 1957, ed. Nowak).

Mass in E minor, for eight-part chorus and wind instruments (1866; revised 1869, 1876 and 1882; pub. 1896; revision of 1882 pub. 1940, ed. Hass and Nowak, and 1959, ed. Nowak).

Mass in F minor, for soloists, chorus, orchestra and organ (1867–8; revised 1872, 1876, 1877, 1881, 1883, and 1890–3; pub. 1894; revision of 1881 pub. 1944, ed. Haas, and 1960, ed. Nowak—with revisions based on newly discovered MSS.).

Te Deum in C major, for soloists, chorus, orchestra and organ (first draft 1881; final version 1883–4; pub. 1885, and 1962, ed. Nowak).

Psalm 150, for soprano solo, chorus and orchestra (1892; published 1892, and 1964, ed. Grasberger).

SMALLER SACRED WORKS

Pange lingua, C major, for four-part chorus (1835 or *c.* 1842; revised 1891).

Tantum ergo, D major, for four-part chorus (1843).

Libera, F major, for four-part chorus and organ (*c.* 1843).

Herz Jesu-Lied, for four-part chorus and organ (authenticity doubtful) (*c.* 1845).

O du liebes Jesukind, for voice and organ (authenticity doubtful) (*c.* 1845).

2 *Asperges me*, for four-part chorus and organ (1845).

5 *Tantum ergo*, in E flat, C, B flat, A flat and D major, for four-part chorus unaccompanied, except No. 5 for five-part chorus with organ (1846; revised 1888; Nos. 1–4 pub. 1888).

Chorale, *Dir Herr, dir will ich mich ergeben*, for four-part chorus (*c.* 1847).

Chorale, *In jener letzten der Nächte*, for four-part chorus (1848).

Tantum ergo, A major, for four-part chorus and organ (*c.* 1848).

Libera, F minor, for five-part chorus, trombones, 'cellos, double bass and organ (1854).

Tantum ergo, B flat major, for four-part chorus, 2 violins and 2 'clarini'[1] (*c.* 1854).

Ave Maria, for solo voices, four-part chorus and organ (1856; pub. in Bruckner's lifetime).

Ave Maria, for seven-part chorus (1861).

Offertory, *Afferentur regi*, for four-part chorus and 3 trombones (1861).

Offertory, *Inveni David*, for male-voice chorus and 4 trombones (1868).

Hymnus, *In St Angelum custodem, Jam lucis orto sidere*, for four-part chorus (Phrygian) (1868; pub. 1868).

Pange lingua, for four-part chorus (Phrygian) (1868; pub. 1885).

[1] The two 'clarini' parts may be horn parts as opposed to trumpet parts.

Asperges me, F major, for four-part chorus (1868).
Locus iste, for four-part chorus (1869; pub. 1886).
Antiphon, *Tota pulchra es Maria*, for tenor, four-part chorus and organ (1878; pub. 1884).
Gradual, *Christus factus est*, for four-part chorus, 3 trombones and 2 violins (1879; revised *c.* 1896; pub. 1886).
Ave Regina (harmonized plainsong) (*c.* 1879).
Gradual, *Os justi*, for four-part chorus (1879; pub. 1886).
Ave Maria, for contralto and organ (1882).
Salvum fac populum, for four-part chorus (1884).
Gradual, *Christus factus est*, for four-part chorus (1884; pub. 1886).
Gradual, *Virga Jesse floruit*, for four-part chorus (1885; pub. 1886).
Ecce sacerdos, for four-part chorus, 3 trombones and organ (1885).
Vexilla regis, for four-part chorus (1892).

ORCHESTRAL WORKS

Apollomarsch, for military band (authenticity doubtful) (1862).
Four Orchestral Pieces (D minor [March], E flat major, E minor and F major)(1862; pub. 1934, ed. Orel).
Overture in G minor (1862–3; pub. 1921, and 1934, ed. Orel).
Symphony in F minor (Study Symphony) (1863; Andante published 1913; piano arrangement pub. 1932; full score pub. 1973, ed. Nowak).
Symphony No. 0 in D minor (1863–4; revised 1869; pub. 1924, ed. Wöss, and 1968, ed. Nowak).
March in E flat major, for military band (1865).
Symphony No. 1 in C minor (1865–6, Linz; revised 1890–1, Vienna; Vienna version pub. 1893, and 1934 in a critical edition by Haas; Linz version pub. 1934, ed. Haas, and 1953, ed. Nowak).
Symphony No. 2 in C minor (1871–2; revised 1876–7 and later, last revision after 1891; pub. 1892; 1872 version pub. 1938, ed. Haas; 1877 version pub. 1965, ed. Nowak).
Symphony No. 3 in D minor (version 1, 1873, unpub.; version 2, 1876–7, pub. 1878, and 1950, ed. Oeser; version 3, 1888–9, pub. 1890, ed. F. Schalk, and 1959, ed. Nowak).
Symphony No. 4 in E flat major ('Romantic') (version 1, 1874;

version 2, 1877–8, with new finale; version 3, 1878–80, with new 'Hunt' scherzo, pub. 1936 and 1944, ed. Haas, and 1953, ed. Nowak; version 4, 1887–8, pub. 1889, ed. F. Schalk and Löwe).

Symphony No. 5 in B flat major (1875–6; slight revisions 1876–8 and later; pub. 1896, ed. F. Schalk, and 1936, ed. Haas, and 1951, ed. Nowak).

Symphony No. 6 in A major (1879–81; pub. 1899, ed. C. Hynais, and 1935, ed. Haas, and 1952, ed. Nowak).

Symphony No. 7 in E major (1881–3; pub. 1885, ed. J. Schalk and Löwe, and 1944, ed. Haas, and 1954, ed. Nowak).

Symphony No. 8 in C minor (1884–7; revised 1887–90; 1890 version pub. 1892, ed. J. Schalk, and 1935 (with many restorations from 1887 version), ed. Haas, and 1955, ed. Nowak; 1887 version pub. 1973 in a critical edition by Nowak).

Symphony No. 9 in D minor (movements 1–3, 1887–94, finale (unfinished) 1894–6; pub. 1903, ed. Löwe, and 1934 (with sketches for the finale) ed. Orel, and 1951, ed. Nowak, and 1963, ed. Schönzeler).

WORKS FOR MIXED CHORUS

Cantata, *Vergissmeinnicht* (Marinelli), for solo quartet, eight-part chorus and piano, three versions (1845).

Cantata, *Entsagen* (from O. Redwitz's 'Amaranth'), with solo voices, chorus and organ or piano (*c.* 1851).

Zwei Totenlieder (1852).

Cantata, *Auf Brüder, auf, zur frohen Feier* (Marinelli), for male-voice quartet, six-part chorus and brass (1852).

Festive song, *St Jodok, Spross aus edlem Stamm,* with solo voices and piano (1855).

Cantata, *Auf Brüder, auf, und die Saiten zur Hand* (Marinelli), for male-voice quartet, male-voice chorus, eight-part mixed chorus, woodwind and brass (1855).

Das edle Herz (Marinelli) (*c.* 1862).

Du bist wie eine Blume (Heine), for solo quartet (1862).

Wahlspruch für den gemischten Chor der Liedertafel Frohsinn in Linz (1868).

WORKS FOR MALE-VOICE CHORUS

An dem Feste (1843) (later *Tafellied*, 1893).
Das Lied vom deutschen Vaterland (*c.* 1845).
Ständchen (*c.* 1846).
Festlied (*c.* 1846).
Der Lehrerstand (*c.* 1847).
Sternschnuppen (*c.* 1848).
Zwei Sängersprüche (1851).
Das edle *Herz* (Marinelli) (*c.* 1851).
Die Geburt (1852).
Vor Arneths Grab, with 3 trombones (1854).
Lasst Jubelklänge laut erklingen (A. Weiss), with brass instruments (1854).
Des Dankes Wort sei mir gegönnt (1855).
Am Grabe (*Grabgesang*) (1861).
Festive Cantata, *Preiset den Herrn* (Pammesberger) for four-part male chorus, woodwind, brass and timpani (1862).
Der Abendhimmel I in A flat major (Zedlitz) (*c.* 1862).
Germanenzug (Silberstein), with brass instruments (1863; published 1865).
Herbstlied (F. Sallet), and with 2 sopranos and piano (1864).
Um Mitternacht I (R. Prutz), with contralto solo and piano (1864).
Trauungslied (Proschko), with organ (1865).
Der Abendhimmel II in F major (Zedlitz), for male quartet only (1866).
O könnt ich dich beglücken (1866).
Vaterländisches Weinlied (Silberstein) (1866).
Wahlspruch für die Liedertafel Sierning (1868).
Mitternacht (J. Mendelssohn), with tenor solo and piano (1870).
Das hohe Lied (Mattig), with 3 soloists and wind band (1876).
Trösterin Musik (A. Seuffert), with organ (1877) (originally called *Nachruf*).
Zur Vermählungsfeier (Silberstein) (1878).
Abendzauber (Mattig), with baritone solo, 3 yodellers and 4 horns (1878).
Sängerbund (Kerschbaum) (1882).
Um Mitternacht II (R. Prutz), with tenor solo (1886).

Träumen und Wachen (Grillparzer), with tenor solo (1890).
Das deutsche Lied (E. Fels), with brass instruments (1892).
Helgoland (Silberstein), with orchestra (1893).

CHAMBER MUSIC

Aequale for 3 trombones (1847).
String Quartet in C minor (1862; pub. 1955, ed. Nowak).
Abendklänge for violin and pianoforte (1866).
String Quintet in F major (1878–9; pub. 1884, and 1963, ed. Nowak).
Intermezzo for string quintet (1879; pub. 1913, and 1963, ed. Nowak).

ORGAN MUSIC

Four Preludes (authenticity doubtful) (*c.* 1836).
Prelude in E flat major (authenticity doubtful) (*c.* 1837).
Prelude and Fugue in D minor (*c.* 1846).
Prelude and Fugue in C minor (1847).
Fugue in D minor (1861).
Prelude in C major, for harmonium (1884).

PIANO MUSIC

Lancier-Quadrille aus beliebten Opernmelodien zusammengestellt (*c.* 1850).
Steiermärker (*c.* 1850).
Three pieces for piano duet (1852–4).
Quadrille for piano duet (*c.* 1854).
Klavierstück in E flat major (*c.* 1856).
Stille Betrachtung an einem Herbstabend (1863).
Erinnerung (*c.* 1868).
Fantasy in G major (1868).

SONGS

Frühlingslied (Heine) (1851).
Amaranths Waldeslieder (O. Redwitz) (*c.* 1858; pub. in *Die Musik*, Berlin, 1902).

Im April (Emanuel Geibel) (*c.* 1868).
Mein Herz und deine Stimme (Platen) (*c.* 1868).
Herbstkummer (Ernst) (*c.* 1868).

SKETCHES

Missa pro Quadragesima, for chorus, organ and trombones (fragments only) (*c.* 1846).
Mass in E flat major, for chorus and orchestra (fragments only) (*c.* 1850).
Student works: First movements to piano sonatas in F major, F minor and G minor, and an *Adagio* for pianoforte in F major (1861–2).
Symphony in B flat major (sketch of 67 bars) (1871).
Requiem in D minor (beginning only) (1875).

LOST WORKS

Domine ad adjuvandum, for chorus and instruments (1835).
Litanei, for chorus and wind instruments (1844).
Salve Regina (1844).
Requiem, for male chorus and organ (1845).
Litanei (*c.* 1856).
Zigeunerwaldlied, for male chorus (1863).

Note Choral works listed above are unaccompanied unless otherwise indicated. Dates of commencement and completion of many works can be found in F. Blume's catalogue in *Musik in Geschichte und Gegenwart*, Vol. 2. The majority of the smaller sacred works, the male-voice choruses and all works for pianoforte and organ are printed in the Göllerich-Auer biography of Bruckner.[1] The sacred motets of 1870–92 were published in Vienna, 1927, ed. E. F. Schmid.[2]

[1] See under Bibliography.

[2] Forthcoming volumes in the Bruckner-Gesellschaft Edition include the *Missa Solemnis* and a volume of Shorter Sacred Works.

Appendix C Personalia

Adler, Guido (1855–1941), Austrian musicologist, born in Moravia. Reader in musical history at the German University of Prague and succeeded E. Hanslick in the chair for music at the University of Vienna (1898–1927). Founder and chief editor of the *Denkmaler der Tonkunst in Österreich.* A pupil of Bruckner and also of Dessoff at the Vienna Conservatorium until 1874.

Assmayer, Ignaz (1790–1862), Austrian organist and prolific composer of oratorios, Masses and other music for the Roman Church. A pupil of Michael Haydn and a friend of Schubert. Appointed court organist at Vienna in 1825 and succeeded Weigl as second court conductor in 1846.

Auer, Max (1880–1962), Austrian biographer of Bruckner. He completed the official biography begun by August Göllerich and wrote other studies of the composer.

Decsey, Ernst (1870–1941), German author and music critic, pupil of Bruckner and Robert Fuchs. He published biographies of Bruckner, Johann Strauss, Wolf and Debussy.

Dessoff, Otto (1835–92), German conductor and composer. After conducting in various small towns from 1854 to 1860 he became conductor at the Vienna Opera, a professor at the Vienna Conservatorium and chief conductor of the Philharmonic concerts in Vienna. After 1875 he occupied similar positions in Karlsruhe and Frankfurt on Main. His daughter, Margarethe Dessoff, moved to New York in 1923 where she founded the Dessoff Choir. He appreciated Bruckner the organist but failed to understand him as a composer.

Dürrnberger, August (1800–80), teacher of music at Linz and author of a book on musical theory. From 1841 he taught Bruckner harmony and thorough-bass and played an important part in securing Bruckner's post as organist of Linz Cathedral.

Eckstein, Friedrich (1861–1939), pupil and friend of Bruckner, a notable musical amateur and a 'character' in Viennese musical circles at the turn of the century. He published a valuable memoir of Bruckner the teacher.

Führer, Robert (1807–61), organist and composer of music for the Roman Church who held posts at Prague, Gmunden, Ischl and Vienna. He composed about 100 Masses. Lost his position in Prague owing to his irregular life, and his doubtful honesty is revealed in an attempt he made to pass off a Mass of Schubert's as his own having added trumpets and drums to it.

Göllerich, August (1859–1923), pupil, friend and official biographer of Bruckner. Also friend and biographer of Liszt. He performed many of Bruckner's early works after the composer's death.

Haas, Robert (1886–1960), Austrian musicologist and editor of Bruckner's works in their original versions. He also edited music of the early seventeenth century and many valuable issues of the Austrian Denkmäler. A distinguished scholar, he was a member of Vienna University and director of the music section of the Vienna State Library. In 1934 he published a fine study of Bruckner.

Hellmesberger, Joseph (1828–93), Austrian conductor, violinist, teacher, wit and leader of a famous string quartet. An infant prodigy, he was a member of a family of fine string-players which spanned three generations. He was director of the Vienna Conservatorium of the Gesellschaft der Musikfreunde (from 1851 on) and conducted that society until 1859. In 1877 he was appointed chief *Kapellmeister* to the Emperor. His performances of Beethoven's late quartets were among the first to awaken interest in those works. Bruckner taught at the Conservatorium under Hellmesberger's direction and Hellmesberger took an erratic interest in his music, commissioning the Quintet.

Herbeck, Johann (1831–77), Austrian conductor and composer. He succeeded Hellmesberger as conductor of the Gesellschafts-konzerte in 1859, became associated with the Vienna Opera in 1863 and its director in 1870. He resigned from the latter post in 1875 owing to continual intrigues. He discovered the original score of Schubert's Unfinished Symphony of which he gave the first performance in 1865. Herbeck was responsible for Bruckner's appointment in Vienna and was one of his most ardent supporters.

Hynais, Cyril, pupil of Bruckner and editor of some of his works. A faithful disciple, he witnessed Bruckner's last will, acted as his copyist during the last years and edited the posthumous publications of Symphony No. 6 and the Andante of the early F minor Symphony.

Kalbeck, Max (1850–1921), Austrian music critic, translator of opera librettos and author of the first full-scale biography of Brahms. He was an unrelenting, hostile critic of Bruckner.

Kattinger, Anton, organist at St Florian and Bruckner's first organ teacher. Bruckner succeeded him in that post in 1855.

Kitzler, Otto (1834–1915), German cellist and conductor. Bruckner studied form and orchestration with him in Linz (1861–3). He was a progressive musician and an early champion of Wagner, whose *Tannhäuser* he first conducted at Linz. In later years he taught and conducted at Brno.

Krismann, Franz Xaver (1726–95), notable Austrian organ builder, born in Carniola. He constructed the great organ at St Florian, completing it in 1774. It was rebuilt by M. Mauracher (1873–5). A restoration of the original organ was completed in 1951.

Lachner, Franz (1803–90), Bavarian conductor, prolific composer and pupil of Sechter. His distinguished career as a conductor culminated in his appointment as Court *Kapellmeister* in Munich (1852). This was terminated prematurely in 1865 because of his antagonism to Wagner. His suites and symphonies achieved great success during his lifetime.

Levi, Hermann (1839–1900), German conductor, originally a friend of Brahms, later on much associated with Wagner, whose *Parsifal* he premiered in 1882. In later years he became one of the first leading conductors genuinely interested in Bruckner's music. His notable Mozart interpretations (edition of *Così fan tutte*) anticipated the Mozart revival of this century. He was conductor of the Court Theatre, Munich, 1872–96.

Löwe, Ferdinand (1865–1925), Austrian conductor, pupil and disciple of Bruckner. In 1883 he became a piano teacher at the Vienna Conservatorium and in 1897 conductor of the Kaim Orchestra, Munich. He edited and published Bruckner's Symphony No. 9 and gave its first performance in 1903.

Mottl, Felix (1856–1911), Austrian conductor and composer, pupil of Bruckner. Much associated with performances of Wagner at Bayreuth and elsewhere. Towards the end of a distinguished and successful career he was appointed director of the Opera at Munich (1907).

Nikisch, Arthur (1855–1922), distinguished Austro-Hungarian conductor. Pupil of Hellmesberger and Dessoff. After some years as an orchestral violinist he took up his chosen career, being appointed first conductor of the Leipzig Opera. Later he was associated with the Leipzig Gewandhaus Orchestra, the Budapest Opera, the Boston Symphony Orchestra and the Philharmonic Concerts in Hamburg. He toured widely. An early admirer of Bruckner, he was a notable interpreter of the symphonies.

Nowak, Leopold (born 1904), Austrian musicologist. He was a pupil of Robert Haas (q.v.), whom he succeeded in 1945 as director of the music section of the Austrian National Library in Vienna. He has issued his own critical Complete Edition of Bruckner's works.

Ochs, Siegfried (1858–1929), German choral conductor. He founded the Philharmonic Choir in Berlin and gave early and successful performances of Bruckner's *Te Deum* and of choral works by Wolf and Reger. He was sincerely attached to Bruckner in the 1890s.

Pachmann, Vladimir de (1848–1933), Russian pianist of Austrian descent. Pupil of Bruckner. Noted exponent of Chopin with a strongly individualistic and often eccentric style.

Richter, Hans (1843–1916), Austro-Hungarian conductor. Associated with Brahms and later wih Wagner. An important early interpreter of Bruckner.

Rott, Hans (1859–?1881), Austrian organist and favourite pupil of Bruckner. He was appointed organist of the Piaristenkirche, Vienna, in 1877 at which time he was a close friend of Mahler. He died in a lunatic asylum.

Schalk, Franz (1863–1931), Austrian conductor. He was Bruckner's pupil and most ardent follower, exercising at times great influence on the ageing composer, whose Symphony No. 5 he edited, first performed (1894) and published after Bruckner's death. He was intimately associated with the Vienna Opera for over thirty years, first as Mahler's assistant (in 1900) and finally as artistic director from 1918 (until 1924 in collaboration with Richard Strauss). Also conductor of the Gesellschaftskonzerte in Vienna for many years, specializing in the works of Bruckner and Mahler. His memoirs, published posthumously in 1935, contain valuable data of Bruckner's life and work.

Schalk, Joseph (1857–1901), pupil of Bruckner and brother of above. His influence on Bruckner was even greater. He advanced the cause of Bruckner by means of piano arrangements, lectures, programme notes and pamphlets. He also championed the music of Wolf.

Seidl, Anton (1850–98), Austro-Hungarian conductor. Appointed conductor of German opera at the New York Metropolitan Opera (1885) and of the New York Philharmonic Society (1891). He gave the first performance of Dvořák's Symphony 'From the New World' in 1893, and the first American performances of several Bruckner symphonies.

Traumihler, Ignaz (1825–84), *Regens Chori* of St Florian from 1852, a Cecilianist and a friend of Bruckner, who dedicated the four-part 'Ave Maria' and the Gradual 'Os justi' to him.

Weinwurm, Rudolf (1835–1911), Austrian choirmaster and composer. A close friend of Bruckner, especially during the Linz period, and he helped prepare the way for Bruckner in Vienna. He founded the Akademische Gesangverein in Vienna (1858) and was appointed firstly choral instructor (1862) and later musical director (1880) of the University. As an inspector of music he did much to raise the standard of musical education in state-subsidized schools and colleges.

Weiss, Johann Baptist (1813–50), composer, organist and teacher at Hörsching, near Linz. He was a first cousin to Bruckner, his mother being a sister of Bruckner's father. In 1833 he became Bruckner's godfather and was his teacher from 1835 to 1837. His Masses and other small liturgical works were important models for Bruckner during his early years of composition. He committed suicide.

Witt, Franz Xaver (1834–88), Catholic priest and composer of sacred music. In 1867 he founded the Caecilienverein, the aim of which was the improvement of Roman Catholic Church music, the restoration of a Palestrinian *a cappella* style, and the total exclusion of the orchestra from devotional music. He edited the periodical *Musica Sacra,* which published in 1885 Bruckner's 'Tantum ergo' and 'Pange lingua' of 1868.

Wöss, Joseph Venantius von (1863–1943), Austrian composer and music-teacher. He edited, published and made piano arrangements of many works by Bruckner. He knew Bruckner and wrote a memoir of him.

Zenetti, Leopold von, organist and music-teacher at Enns, Upper Austria. He taught Bruckner from 1843 to 1846.

Appendix D Bibliography

The following list makes no attempt to include all the literature on Bruckner, and refers only to books and articles of importance to this volume. Of the studies in English, the books of Doernberg and Schönzeler contain admirable biographies, whilst Simpson's 'The Essence of Bruckner' is a most readable and penetrating analytical approach to the symphonies for the reader who has some knowledge of score-reading and harmony. Among the more scholarly writings in German the books by Auer, Haas, Nowak and Orel are strongly recommended. The four-volume study of Göllerich and Auer is the standard work on Bruckner: it contains a wealth of detailed information not found elsewhere.

Auer, Max, *Anton Bruckner, sein Leben und Werk* (6th ed., Vienna, 1966).

Blume, F., article 'Bruckner' in *Die Musik in Geschichte und Gegenwart*, Vol. 2 (Cassel, 1952).

Bruckner, Anton, *Gesammelte Briefe*, ed. Gräflinger and Auer, 2 vols (Regensburg, 1924).

Vorlesungen über Harmonielehre und Kontrapunkt, ed. E. Schwanzara (Vienna, 1951).

Brunner, Franz, *Dr Anton Bruckner* (Linz, 1895).

Chord and Discord, 'Journal of the Bruckner Society of America' (1932 fol.).

Cooke, Deryck, 'The Bruckner Problem simplified' (*Musical Times*, Jan., Feb., Apr., May and Aug. 1969).

Article, 'Bruckner' in Grove's *Dictionary*, sixth edition.

Dawson-Bowling, Paul, 'Thematic and tonal unity in Bruckner's Eighth Symphony' (*Music Review*, August 1969).

Decsey, Ernst, *Bruckner: Versuch eines Lebens* (Berlin, 1920).
Dehnert, Max, *Anton Bruckner, Versuch einer Deutung* (Leipzig, 1958).
Doernberg, Erwin, *The life and symphonies of Anton Bruckner* (London, 1960).
Eckstein, F., *Erinnerungen an Anton Bruckner* (Vienna, 1924).
Gallois, Jean, *Bruckner* (Paris, 1971).
Göllerich, August, and Auer, Max, *Anton Bruckner*, 4 vols (Regensburg, 1922–36).
Gräflinger, Franz, *Anton Bruckner* (Berlin, 1927).
Liebes und Heiteres um Anton Bruckner (Vienna, 1948).
Grüninger, Fritz, *Anton Bruckner: der metaphysische Kern seiner Persönlichkeit und Werke* (Augsburg, 1930).
Der Ehrfürchtige: Anton Bruckners Leben dem Volke erzählt (Freiburg i.B., 1937).
Der Meister von Sankt Florian—Wege zu Anton Bruckner (Augsburg, 1950).
Haas, Robert, *Anton Bruckner* (Potsdam, 1934).
Halm, August, *Die Symphonie Anton Bruckners* (Munich, 1923).
Hruby, C., *Meine Erinnerungen an Anton Bruckner* (Vienna, 1901).
Klose, Friedrich, *Meine Lehrjahre bei Bruckner* (Regensburg, 1927).
Krohn, I., *Anton Bruckners Symphonien: Untersuchung über Formenbau und Stimmungsgehalt*, 3 vols (Helsinki, 1955–7).
Kurth, Ernst, *Bruckner*, 2 vols (Berlin, 1925).
Lassl, Josef, *Das kleine Brucknerbuch* (Salzburg, 1965).
Linninger, F., *Orgeln und Organisten im Stift St Florian* (Linz, 1955).
Machabey, Armand, *La Vie et l'œuvre d'Anton Bruckner* (Paris, 1945).
Newlin, Dika, *Bruckner-Mahler-Schoenberg* (New York, 1947).
Nowak, Leopold, *Anton Bruckner, Musik und Leben* (Vienna, 1964).
Oeser, Fritz, *Die Klangstruktur der Bruckner-Symphonie* (Leipzig, 1939).
Orel, Alfred, *Anton Bruckner, das Werk, der Künstler, die Zeit* (Vienna, 1925).
Anton Bruckner, sein Leben in Bildern (Vienna, 1936).
Bruckner Brevier (Vienna, 1953).
Raynor, H., 'An Approach to Anton Bruckner' (*Musical Times*, Feb. 1955).

Redlich, H. F., 'The Finale of Bruckner's Ninth Symphony' (*Monthly Musical Record*, July–Aug. 1949).
Reich, Willi, *Anton Bruckner—ein Bild seiner Persönlichkeit* (Basel, 1953).
Schalk, Franz, *Briefe und Betrachtungen* (Vienna, 1935).
Schönzeler, Hans-Hubert, *Bruckner* (London, 1970).
Schwanzara, Erich, *Anton Bruckners Stamm und Urheimat* (Regensburg, 1937).
Simpson, Robert, *Bruckner and the symphony* (London, 1963).
The Essence of Bruckner (London, 1967).
Tschulik, Norbert, *Anton Bruckner im Spiegel seiner Zeit* (Vienna, 1965).
Vassenhove, Leon van, *Anton Bruckner* (Neuchatel, 1942).
Wehle, G. F., *Anton Bruckner im Spiegel seiner Zeitgenossen* (Garmisch-Partenkirchen, 1964).

NOTE ON RECORDINGS

Whereas a complete discography would be impractical in a book of this kind, owing to the continual changes in the catalogues of record companies, a brief list of the most important performances available on disc might be helpful.

Of the great interpreters of former years, Wilhelm Furtwängler and Bruno Walter stand to the fore. Furtwängler's recordings of Bruckner's Symphonies are available on H.M.V., Electrola, Deutsche Grammophon and Unicorn. Deeply moving performances of the Fourth, Seventh and Ninth Symphonies by Walter are on C.B.S. Another monumental performance of No. 9 is that of Carl Schuricht (Classics for Pleasure label) while Otto Klemperer is represented on Columbia. George Szell has a fine performance of the Third Symphony (1889 version) on C.B.S.

Both Bernard Haitink (Philips) and the Eugen Jochum (Deutsche Grammophon) have issued recordings of the complete Bruckner symphonies. Jochum has also recorded most of the sacred choral works and other sacred works are available under John Alldis, George Guest and Roger Norrington on the Argo label. The Keller Quartet have recorded the String Quartet, Quintet and Intermezzo (on Oryx) and Hans-Hubert Schönzeler has made the first recordings of some early Bruckner works on the Unicorn label.

Index

Index